Your
Marvelous
Mind

Also by
Michael Grant

Beyond Blame

Your
Marvelous
Mind

**Motivational Power
for Meaningful Living**

Michael Grant

HILLSBORO PRESS
Franklin, Tennessee

Printed in the United States of America

04   03   02   01   00   1   2   3   4   5

Library of Congress Catalog Card Number: 00-101545

ISBN: 1-57736-188-1

Cover design by Gary Bozeman

Published by
HILLSBORO PRESS
an imprint of
PROVIDENCE HOUSE PUBLISHERS
238 Seaboard Lane • Franklin, Tennessee 37067
800-321-5692
www.providencehouse.com

To the greater honor and glory of Almighty
God, who is the true Author of all that
inspires and uplifts the human spirit.

and

To my eldest brother, Anthony Lee Grant,
one of my first role models, who taught me
early on to believe in myself.

"I have found power
in the mysteries
of thought."

—Euripedes

Contents

Preface & Acknowledgments

THIS BOOK IS ABOUT UNDERSTANDING HUMAN BEHAVIOR—specifically, your own. Hopefully, you will gain some insights that will allow you to more closely examine the origins of your behavior and to question whether any particular aspect of your behavior is adding or subtracting from the quality of your life. Here are a series of essays designed to assist you in your personal evolution towards a life filled with more joy and satisfaction.

One great thinker warned us that life is the toughest school of all. The reason? In life, we get the tests first and wait for the lessons to come later. The chief purpose of this book is to assure you that you need not feel defenseless as you confront life's myriad tests. This book will serve as a silent partner and friendly coach as you set out to learn life's endless lessons.

Like the decathlon athlete or the scholar in pursuit of a higher understanding of academic principles, you will have your mettle tried every day. In his famous book, *The Road Less Traveled*, Dr. M. Scott Peck stated: "Life is hard." I believe Dr. Peck's statement is only partially true. Life is hard—and much, much more. It is also exhilarating, challenging, shocking, absorbing, revealing, mind-boggling, and beautiful. Each day that we live we are called upon to redefine ourselves and recommit to some purpose far greater than ourselves.

Again resembling the world-class athlete or the determined student, we are continuously asked to stretch beyond our reach. We are called to come out of our comfort zones for growth's sake. We are reminded daily that the elusive happiness that all of us seek can only be found when we decide to help bring it to others. We also experience varying degrees of happiness while working on such worthwhile goals. We are most fulfilled when we are using our brains to make good things happen for ourselves and others. Our brains have a cybernetic functioning capability. We are always working either to advance some far-reaching goal or to satisfy a more immediate one.

If we bothered to study the lessons of those who have gone before us, we would benefit from the wisdom of those thoughtful souls who taught us by their words and deeds how to use our human potential to attain desirable levels of personal satisfaction. The great ones, who left "their footprints on the sands of time," left many blueprints for purposeful living. Their contributions to the collective experience of our species have taught us—if we paid close attention—that there are no free lunches. It is all about effort. It is all about direction. It is all about taking personal responsibility for the countless choices that each of us will make over the course of a lifetime.

There are no easy fixes. Why even discuss whether or not life has been fair? We are simultaneously victims of caprice and beneficiaries of countless blessings. The cause for hope (for those who can comprehend the universal law of mental attraction) is: whatever you really believe that life will do to or for you, you will see it come to pass.

Upon being asked how to get to Mount Olympus, Socrates reputedly said: "Make sure that each step that you take is in that direction." You have been given the greatest gift bestowed on any species within the animal kingdom—your marvelous mind. You now know that you can guide or misguide its awesome power according to the thoughts that you consciously choose to direct your course. If the metaphor of Mount Olympus means anything to you (i.e., more health, more wealth, a greater contribution to the well-being of our species, a greater reverence for the planet that nurtures us, or simply a mind that is more at peace), just follow the wisdom of Socrates and make sure that every step is taken in that direction.

It is always difficult to justly recognize everyone who helped you to accomplish some task that you deemed important. *Your Marvelous Mind* is truly the by-product of too many countless decent men and women to recall by name.

The following is, at best, a partial listing of those wonderful human beings who helped me to develop a philosophy of true grit and tough-minded optimism.

First, I would like to extend boundless gratitude to my business partner and great friend, Victor Cook. Vic's organized mind, incredible dedication, and belief in the business enterprise that gave birth to *Your Marvelous Mind* all make him nearly a co-author. He guarded over the project from beginning to end, never doubting for a moment that it would come to fruition.

Next, to my mother, Mrs. Verleon Smithson-Grant, who went beyond the call of duty to become a non-stop source of inspiration and support.

To my first publisher, Sr. Sandra Smithson, I can honestly say that this second book is possible because of the first effort. Sister Sandra's work to reach "the least of these" continues to inspire me to follow her leadership.

To Dorcas Alley, my mentor for six years, I owe a great debt of gratitude. She taught me to write, to speed-read, and to speak passionately.

John Seigenthaler, founder of the Freedom Forum and First Amendment Center at Vanderbilt University, has opened so many doors for writers and community activists.

I would also like to thank my brother Attorney Charles K. Grant for overcrowding his hectic schedule to find time to edit the manuscript. Also, to Robyn Clark, motivation editor for *Black Enterprise Magazine*, I owe a debt of gratitude for her thorough editing of the manuscript as well.

And lastly, I would like to thank the creative staff at Providence House Publishers for their huge effort that finally brought this book to you, the reader. They are a great team.

Your
Marvelous
Mind

Introduction

ANGLO-IRISH SATIRIST JONATHAN SWIFT SAID IT BEST: "MAY you live all the days of your life." His blessing summoned up the entire message of this book, which has been written with a simple objective: to encourage every reader—and every person whom the reader may choose to touch—to make an honest, daily effort to live each day to the fullest.

The goal of being fully alive every day, regardless of circumstances (i.e., the weather, the reality of death, betrayals of our sacred trust, persistent fears, heartbreaking setbacks, the accelerated pace of change as a perennial phenomenon, doubts, worries, and far too many instances of man's inhumanity to man), is not only the real challenge for all of us but also the ultimate reward and guaranteed way to find meaning in our lives.

Hopefully, this motivational book will deviate somewhat from the well-worn path of many in its genre. While it will clearly advocate a preference for tough-minded (not to be confused with Pollyannaish) optimism, it will not gloss over life's "aridity and disenchantment" to rush the reader towards some hyped-up, ethereal high. Neither easy solutions for successful living nor get-rich-quick schemes will be advanced. Instead, the reader will be encouraged to participate actively in the learning process that unfolds as he or she reads each new essay. Questions at the essay's end will provide the reader with many opportunities to be an actor, not merely a spectator. The questions have been painstakingly framed to engage both hemispheres of one's brain, the logical and analytical left as well as the holistic and creative right. The questions also challenge the reader not to focus solely on the author's perspective but rather to expand one's own consciousness by observing of one's own perspective. Ideally, the questions should stimulate a person's question-generating abilities. Albert Einstein once stated: "Genius comes more from bold questions than from finding right answers." One of the goals of this book is to introduce or reintroduce each reader to the genius that resides within himself or herself. By choosing to gloss over the questions, he or she will no doubt minimize the impact that the essay could have on the process of unleashing the genius that wants to be liberated.

Your Marvelous Mind is the small but honest effort of one writer to share a less than perfect prescription for achieving whatever degree of success (however you define it) one's heart desires. To this end, a candid discussion about the most powerful weapon that each person possesses—the human mind—hopefully will cause the reader to make a paradigmatic shift and to begin to reframe his or her existing thoughts and present perceptions about how to live life to its fullest.

This book, borrowing a bit from the work of the father of psychoanalytic thought, Dr. Sigmund Freud, will attempt at least a cursory discussion of the profound implications of what he believed to be the existence of a powerfully motivating yet hidden, unconscious mind. To the extent that each person can become aware that humans are often shoved in one direction or another—oftentimes to their detriment—by a covert mind avoiding the scrutiny of conscious awareness, one becomes better able to take preemptive, defensive action in going about the serious business of trying to enjoy rather than merely endure our daily existence.

In the second section, the reader will be reminded of the existence of the most powerful counteroffensive to the unconscious mind's ever-present destruction capability, the boundless and resourceful subconscious mind. It has been called the universal mind, infinite intelligence, and the superconscious mind. Some from the world of metaphysics have even suggested that our subconscious mind is literally our direct, spiritual, and mental link to the mind of that guiding force of the universe, Almighty God.

It is believed by many that the subconscious mind, when understood and properly reprogrammed, is able to produce the solutions to all of life's problems. The subconscious mind—that deep reservoir filled with habitual thoughts and feelings—acts as a moment-by-moment architect of the building process called daily human experience. Most incredible is the fact that the vast majority of men and women live their entire lives without really understanding or using for their own enrichment the ever-present power of their subconscious minds. Yet, this need not be everyone's fate.

The subconscious mind's problem-solving capabilities are enormous. It has been estimated that the subconscious mind can compute over one hundred thousand times faster than the conscious mind. Earl Nightengale, a famous proponent of the human mind's unlimited potential, once stated: "We become what we think about all day long. We get what we focus our thoughts on." If one understands that any idea or thought which is received into the subconscious mind as true, be it good or evil, productive or destructive, leading to happiness or to misery, then it becomes, for all practical purposes, part of one's living reality; that person becomes aware of the awesome power of choice that is always available.

The strangling effects of fear demonstrate how powerful the subconscious mind is. Many of our phobias (e.g., fear of flying, fear of public speaking, claustrophobia, fear of insects, fear of snakes, etc.) are constant reminders that we have created beneath the surface of our conscious awareness habitual, stimulus-response reactions to things and situations that may represent no cause for alarm for others. Many psychologists believe that traumatic childhood experiences are probably the root causes of many of our deep-rooted fears. Successful therapy—or desensitizing ourselves from the painful effects of these fears—must always involve some process of challenging their truthfulness or soundness, coupled with a refilling of the mind's belief fountain. But knowing that these fears—which have been accepted as real threats in the subconscious mind—can be programmed out restores a sense of confidence and freedom to daily living.

If the subconscious mind is the pilot guiding us from one nightmarish fear to another, it is also the faithful genie who delivers life's greatest treasures (i.e., love, wealth, health, a sense of accomplishment, and much more).

The terms *subconscious* and *unconscious* are often used interchangeably. For purposes of clarification, the subconscious mind can be defined as that part of the mind that is reprogrammable while the unconscious mind serves as the storehouse for an individual's most primeval instincts or primitive drives. Many of our most destructive impulses are repressed in the unconscious mind. Without attempting to reach beyond my own comprehension of Freud's theory of the unconscious mind or Dr. Joseph Murphy's explanation of the subconscious mind, throughout this book the term *unconscious* will be used to refer to human motives that are characteristically hidden from one's conscious awareness, and the term *subconscious* used to represent that ingenious ability which is built upon and activated by habitual patterns and strongly held beliefs. The subconscious mind represents what is accepted to be true. It has been stated that self-concept (how one thinks and feels about oneself) is the subconscious mind's master plan.

After exploring the layers of the mind or levels of consciousness, the reader will then be invited to take a second look at many of the common themes that fill the pages of most motivational books: the importance of purposeful living, goal setting, creative visualization, controlling thoughts, and dealing with such negative feelings as anger, doubt, fear, and rejection.

Before the conclusion, the reader who diligently stayed tuned and actively engaged throughout the book should have in his or her survival kit new tools to help keep the engines of persistence hot while pursuing one's goals, a plan for how to form new, more self-loving habits, and a few useful techniques to help rid oneself of all the *should*s, *ought to*s, and *have to*s that constantly force people to try to live in some reality other than the one presently before them.

Other topics designed to add to the richness of the reader's own personal experience are also covered, and are written with the same intent: to guide the reader, by clear and convincing evidence, to the ineluctable conclusion that by exercising proper scrutiny over those thoughts and emotions which often dominate human beings, one can (to paraphrase John Milton's popular saying) create not a hell of heaven but a heaven of hell.

Before the reader begins to lose himself or herself in the thoughts contained herein, please be forewarned by the great wisdom found in these anonymous, but famous words: "After all is said and done, it is not what we think or feel. Ultimately what matters is what we do."

Five Foundational Questions

1. *Taking an educated guess, where are you at this present moment on the continuum representing your life?*

Birth ———————————————————— Death

2. *What is your grandest ambition?*

3. *What part of you most inhibits your personal growth?*

4. *Choose one word that describes how you "feel" most people perceive you?*

5. *How have your habitual thought patterns shaped who you are today?*

PART I

"The mind is its own place. It can make hell of heaven or heaven of hell."
—JOHN MILTON

How the
Human Mind Works
Understanding The Power of Both the Conscious and Unconscious Minds

FOR THOSE SEEKING TO TAKE CONTROL OF THEIR DESTINIES, nothing will assist their efforts more than fully grasping the differences between the conscious (aware, logical) mind and the unconscious (unaware) mind.

Freud, the father of psychoanalytic theory, surmised after years of study and clinical observation that human beings are not guided solely by the conscious decisions of the mind of which we are aware. We are also inexorably directed by an incredibly powerful unconscious mind which is lodged deep within the human psyche and functions much like a nonstop tape recorder.

This tape recorder, whose capacity endows each of us with a photographic memory, began collecting data while we were still snugly cradled in our mothers' wombs. Every feeling, every thought, and every occurrence that the individual experiences—overt or subtle—are remembered and stored in the unconscious mind.

The conscious mind is the order-giver. The conscious mind has no memory capacity; it simply judges, wills, and decides. Affirmations emanate from the conscious mind. Whatever comes to our awareness through the five senses and/or our present thoughts constitute components of the conscious mind.

An easy, if somewhat inept, analogy would be what you observe after you pour a glass of Coke or Pepsi. The dark part—the concentrated essence of the soda—represents the unconscious mind. The more ephemeral, foamy substance at the top of the glass would represent the conscious mind. Conscious thoughts are fleeting; unconscious thoughts are stored indefinitely.

Dr. Carl Jung, a contemporary of Freud, took it one step further. He hypothesized that not only do individuals have both a conscious and unconscious mind, but so do groups of people. So, for example, the thoughts and feelings that construct the personal identities or self-concepts (i.e., what we think and feel about ourselves) of individuals may be multiplied to reflect what groups think and feel about themselves or about reality in general.

To begin the process of reprogramming our minds and elevating our individual and group self-esteem, we should consider the following information.

It has been estimated that between twenty thousand and fifty thousand thoughts will run through your head every day. Some psychologists have estimated that as much as 87 percent of our habitual thinking is negative. On a typical day, many of us are bombarded with worries, doubts, and fears that literally drain our energies and leave us feeling somewhat overwhelmed at best, and desperate at worst.

In his enlightening book, *Maximum Achievement*, Brian Tracy has estimated that 95 percent of our actions and reactions are automatic, unconscious responses to our physical and human environment.

By first becoming aware of our silent, but incredibly powerful thoughts and feelings, and then by observing the behavior that is their by-product, we arm ourselves by consciously sending emotionally-charged, positive counterstatements to the subconscious mind. Eventually, these new commands will take root and cause modifications in our behavior.

Next, listen intently to the nonstop, internal conversation that you have with yourself. Then, ask yourself whether or not you are making matters worse than they really are. If so, you will literally need to interrupt negative thoughts and replace them with ones that create hope and boost energy.

It is important to decide as soon as possible what you think your purpose in life is. If necessary, spend days, weeks or months contemplating what your role in the cosmic plan must be. Once your purpose has been revealed to you, seek to order your thoughts in such a way that everything you do moves you closer to the fulfillment of your life's calling.

These thoughts will be discussed in more detail later in this book. For now, if you have a better understanding of the different aspects of the human mind and how your beliefs and ultimately your behavior are affected by these different mental layers, you will be able to take control of how their awesome power is shading your view of reality—your perspective about what is and is not possible for your life.

Questions

1. How does monitoring your behavior help to expose unconscious self-sabotage?

2. Albert Einstein once said: "It's not what we see, it's what we see with." How might your overall attitude about life be "colored" by what you see with?

3. In *Even Eagles Need A Push*, David McNally suggested: "In order to get what you want, you must first know what you want and then really want what you want." In light of your understanding of the unconscious mind and the power of habit, why do you suppose an intensity of desire is needed in your quest to overcome thoughts of limitation (e.g., "I'm too old"; "I don't have the funds to get started"; "What if I fail?"; "What's the use? I tried before and failed"; "I'm not smart enough"; "Some people are just luckier than I am", etc.)?

4. Many individuals who try to get a larger vision of what's possible for their lives become overwhelmed by feelings of inadequacy or become shackled by fears of failure or rejection. How might you deal with the emotional discomfort that always accompanies a departure from your comfort zone?

5. Identify two challenges that you must face and overcome in order to become emotionally and physically healthier. Construct a written strategy. (Note: remember that self-acceptance must be the first step in your plan to become healthier emotionally.)

 THINK THE RIGHT THOUGHTS

HAVE YOU EVER WONDERED WHY SOME INDIVIDUALS CAN BE born with the proverbial silver spoon in their mouths, cradled in the lap of luxury, and given every means of support only to end up as skid row bums? Yet, others can be born and raised in abject poverty, but somehow manage to amass great wealth, develop their minds to the point of sheer brilliance, and give this world another model of excellence to emulate.

What is the ever-present catalyst that guides the chain of events that culminates into the thing called destiny? The answer is found in the realm of human thoughts. That is where the power is, or more simply stated: at any existential moment of your life, you are a reflection of your dominant, persistent thoughts. Acceptance of this truth can transform your life forever. But please be forewarned by the great thinker who concluded: "We are not our thoughts; and our thoughts are not reality. We are the thinker of our thoughts and our thoughts are only our perception of reality."

> *"A single thought.*
> *A few micromilliwatts*
> *of energy flowing*
> *through our brains.*
> *A seemingly*
> *innocuous, almost*
> *ephemeral thing.*
> *And yet . . . "*
>
> —JOHN ROGER AND
> PETER MCWILLIAMS

What is the difference? If you know you are not your thoughts, you have the advantage of doing two things that many may not think to exercise as options:

1. You can stop identifying with negative thoughts about yourself and suffering the painful side-effects resulting from them; and

2. You can ignore those thoughts that lead you away from what it is you want to accomplish or enjoy.

For example, if a young lady has encountered a series of relationships with lovers who have treated her badly, more likely than not, she will begin to develop emotional defenses to protect herself from future abusive situations.

Her thoughts, springing from the well of her emotions, may sound something like this inside her head: "No one is going to hurt me again," or "You can't trust men," or "All men are dogs," or "I can be miserable by myself, I don't need help to be miserable."

If the young lady has the awareness that she is not her thoughts and that her thoughts are not reality—that she is, instead, the thinker of her thoughts and her thoughts are just her perception of reality—she is better able to disrupt the painful pattern of her past. By conscious design, she creates distance between herself and those energy-draining, self-defeating thoughts.

Since she is the thinker of her thoughts, or what Dr. Deepak Chopra would call "the silent, intelligent knower behind the thoughts"—the creator of those thoughts—she becomes aware that between each thought there are a million possibilities or choices of other thoughts that she can select to explain her predicament to herself.

First, to get control of her undesirable situation, she must interrupt a predictable train of negative, generalized thinking that only exacerbates her condition by making things seem worse than they really are.

Next, she could tap into the unlimited power of her mind by consciously choosing simply to tell herself the truth. Are all men really dogs? Is it true that you cannot trust any man? Have you ever met a man anywhere on this planet that you could trust? There are over one billion adult males on this planet; surely one of them can be trusted.

Next, she begins to empower herself when she chooses to free herself from the *victim syndrome* by acknowledging that she was possibly a coconspirator in the love plots that resulted in her dilemma. She can choose to take responsibility for her role in the mistreatment/degradation pattern. Is it not true that people treat us the way we "train them to treat us?" If we make doormats of ourselves, others will walk on us.

Moving from victim to victor, she now takes high command by choosing to expand her limited perception of reality (i.e., "the men that I have dealt with treated me badly") in order to create a wider perception (i.e., "of the millions of men whom I have not met, maybe there is one who will love and respect me").

> "We are the thinker of our thoughts and our thoughts are only our perception of reality."

When one becomes aware of his or her private thoughts, of the conversation that goes on nonstop in his or her head, that individual suddenly realizes that the events in his or her life—love issues, money issues, friendship issues, etc.—mostly reflect what we tell ourselves with the thoughts that we allow to dominate our minds.

Unfortunately, for a great number of us, most of our thoughts are self-defeating. They work against our own best interest. Psychologists tell us that of the some fifty thousand thoughts (give or take a few thousand) that run through our heads each day about 87 percent of them are negative! We constantly tell ourselves what we cannot have, who we are not, who does not love us, who we cannot trust, what we do not like, how impossible or unlikely something is, what we do not have to work with, and how hard and stressful life is.

Those who are enjoying life, in spite of its many obstacles, have learned that what is happening "out there" (our experiences) is generally a reflection of what is going on "in here" (our thoughts). It has been written that everything is created twice: first in the mind and then in reality. It is the universal law of cause and effect at work.

So, now that you know how powerful those thoughts are and that you can control them (and you may have known all this before you began reading this book or before I knew it), have some fun with your power.

Want to go back to school to get that college degree or master's degree or a doctorate? *Thought:* Why not? Want to start that little business on the side or expand your present one tenfold? *Thought:* Others have done it with no more intelligence or resources than I have. Want to leave a job where your best efforts are not appreciated? *Thought:* I'm probably wasting my energy and creativity when I could invest it somewhere else or with someone who would appreciate my efforts. Want to have a love life that sparkles with affection and is guided by true love and respect? *Thought:* If it has happened for others with no more attractiveness, education, or pleasing personality than I have, it can happen for me. In short, use a powerful affirmation: it will happen for me!

Get the picture? Think the right thoughts. They are the words that make up the pages in the various parts of the book that is your magnificent life. You are the author and you are the main character.

So will you take pen in hand and write a glorious story? One that will inspire others to see that taking control of their thoughts will cause a change in the way they view reality as well.

A change in thoughts creates a concomitant shift in perception. One begins to abandon a former image of self as a bewildered survivor on a tugboat that is being tossed capriciously about on the stormy seas of life; instead, it is replaced with a far more empowering image of a captain going to the helm of his great ship, skillfully navigating it through life's tidal waves and bringing it safely into port.

Just how much power do thoughts wield? The next essay will answer this question.

Questions

1. Have you ever sat calmly for an hour and just observed your thoughts without reaction or judgment? Try it. You will be fascinated by the experience.

2. How does one stop identifying with or holding onto negative, self-defeating thoughts?

3. If it is true that, on the average, about 87 percent of our thoughts are negative, how does one lower that percentage and tip the scales in favor of a higher percentage of positive, uplifting, inspiring thoughts?

4. Much negative thinking is habitual. How does one retrain himself or herself to interrupt negative thought patterns?

5. What is meant by the statement: "Everything is created twice: first in our minds and then in reality"? What will you create in your mind today that could change your reality forever?

6. Why is a negative mental attitude easier to maintain than a positive mental attitude? Why is negative thinking more costly?

THOUGHTS OF THUNDER
WILL LEAVE YOU SINGING

WIMPY, INCONSISTENT, UNCOMMITTED, WAVERING, WISHY-washy, equivocating, maybe-I-will and maybe-I-will-not thoughts all conspire to limit us, water down our efforts, and force us to settle for mediocre, uneventful, boring, and frustrating moments, hours, days, weeks, months, and years. These anemic thoughts force us off the throne of magnificent living to wallow in the pit of the serf's overcrowded and drudgery-filled dungeon.

So, my friend, let me ask you: Do you recall having experienced powerful thoughts that came with volatile emotions? In this case, I am not alluding to those self-frightening, anxiety-provoking, worry-infested, negative thoughts.

If you are the typical person, you may feel that these self-defeating thoughts are indeed powerful. They are not! They are illusions created by our lower nature to harness our energy into aiding their destructive mission, like health-usurping pathogens that invade our bodies and turn healthy cells against us. But thoughts of thunder generate real power!

We have all experienced the jolting capability of these thoughts of thunder. Sometimes, they appear to us in the form of "a-ha!" or a similar moment of great insight. At other times, they are triggered by the words or deeds of others. *What is certain is this: they are never subtle!*

Thoughts of thunder crackle. They electrocute the enemy within by first identifying the villainous self that tries to rob us of life.

Ordinary thoughts standing alone are insufficient. Ordinary thoughts must be charged with unleashed emotion to become bellowing, attention-grabbing thoughts of thunder. In order to blast ourselves out of our slumps, we must listen to these overpowering thoughts. We need to allow them to roar, to storm, and to unshackle us from the chains of our habitual ways of thinking and doing.

If we will let our thoughts of thunder strike the heart of our comfort zones, we will open a veritable floodgate of new or innovative ways of thinking.

Thoughts of thunder will also shatter our illusions of security which are continually reinforced by going to the same places, seeing the same people, and indulging in the same discussions.

Thoughts of thunder will compel us to move upwards in our thinking processes and begin to question why we keep falling into the same old traps. At this elevated level of consciousness, we start to understand why we persist in making the same mistakes over and over again!

Thoughts of thunder will drench our minds with the urgent reality that time is the most precious commodity that we have; with each moment we possess the option of investing or wasting it. Time may be infinite but our mortal existence clearly is not.

Like flashes of lightning, thoughts of thunder allow us to see beyond the horizon of the obvious to catch a hope-filled glimpse of what is really possible for our lives.

Thoughts of thunder blow off the covers that we use to conceal all the lies we tell ourselves about who we really are and what we really want from life. The late, great Dr. Norman Vincent Peale warned us: "Beware of what you really want, you'll get it everytime."

Many of us talk endlessly about what we value, what we intend to accomplish, and what we believe in. But all too often, our actions paint a different picture of reality. Self-deception is a mortal enemy in the battle for self-fulfillment and must be treated as such.

There is more. Thoughts of thunder will send us through hurricanes of discomfort so that we can begin to see the emerging oasis of what our lives could look like when we decide to stop blaming others for our predicaments. These more majestic thoughts will elevate us to live on a higher plateau, where we stop using the shortcomings of others (mama, daddy, brother, sister, teacher, coach, Whites, Blacks, Jews, or Asian Americans) as excuses for our own failures. It may well be the objective of others to frustrate our efforts but we must remember that ultimately, no one can keep us from receiving what life wants to give us, unless we allow it.

Also, thoughts of thunder can cause tornadoes designed to disconnect us from the poisonous patterns of the past, thereby uprooting the strangling emotions planted by other people's misguided assessments of our innate worth and our acceptance of their miscalculations.

If we are not frightened by them, thoughts of thunder will create an earthquake of destabilization in our psyches, they will ignite a cataclysmic explosion of mountains of doubt, fear, and low self-esteem fossilized by years of negative mental programming (the effects of which are buried deep beneath the surface of an observable reality).

Our salvation—as individuals and as a species—lies in a courageous embracing of our thoughts of thunder. So please, when they come, do not be afraid of them. If they create an emotional crisis, you may need to seek professional help. But for the vast majority, they are nonthreatening attempts to present wonderful, life-altering opportunities. At a deeper level of awareness, these forceful thoughts challenge us to let go of a past unworthy of who we really are. In the end, the only thing we stand to lose in the turmoil is the false belief that we are less than we were created to be.

So ride through the storms created by your liberating thoughts of thunder. Their tempestuous winds will sweep your mind clean of the rubbish from a fragmented self.

Are those risks associated with heeding these eye-opening thoughts of thunder worth the effort? The answer is a resounding yes!

I believe we begin to see real opportunities for starting over again, a chance to "get it right" this time. We begin to understand the Biblical wisdom that teaches us that we are more than conquerors.

When we hear the messages communicated in our thoughts of thunder, we soon realize that we are indeed blessed. We start to get "in touch" with our true selves. With clearer filters, our views of what is possible change dramatically. The air is cleaner and all of nature appears more pristine and beautiful.

Looking back, we realize that our thoughts of thunder were both teacher and friend. Among their myriad messages of hope is yet another anonymous, crowning jewel of wisdom which leaves us consoled and inspired with a single lesson: "Little birds sing after a storm, why shouldn't we?"

Questions

1. Have you ever gone to bed heavy-laden with burdens and overwhelmed with problems that seemed irreconcilable, only to wake up feeling refreshed and knowing exactly how you would handle the previous night's dilemmas? What do you suppose happened during your night's rest?

2. The subconscious mind works while we sleep and when we are awake. How would you imagine that you could get it to solve problems for you while you are awake or in the midst of a crisis?

3. Why is courage needed to embrace the helpful messages found in our "bellowing thoughts of thunder"?

4. How would you suppose that your strong intuition might convey an important, possibly life-altering message to you?

HABITS
Where Will Your Autopilot Guide You?

AS STATED IN THE FIRST ESSAY, IT IS ESTIMATED THAT ABOUT 95 percent of our behavior is habitual: spontaneous, unthinking, reactive behavior—a subconscious response to a stimulus.

This means, to a great extent, that each of us are moving through life on automatic pilot. If we are not consciously aware of what we are doing and why we are doing it, we may well be on a collision course. What are your destructive habits?

One great mind once wrote: "Bad habits are easy to form but hard to live with. Good habits are hard to form but easy to live with. Therefore, we should develop good habits and make them our masters." This is great advice, but it's easier said than done.

Where do our habits originate? How do these predictable patterns get a stronghold of our psyches? Why do people resolve to break their bad habits and then break their promises to themselves? And lastly, are there dependable strategies for successfully overcoming bad habits?

I believe that most people do not really understand the origins (or powerful influence) of their bad habits. According to Brian Tracy, author of *Maximum Achievement*, "All habits—positive or negative—are conditioned responses to stimuli. They are learned as the result of repetition, until they are firmly ingrained in the subconscious mind."

Each of us has both a conscious mind (present awareness) and a subconscious mind (unconscious autopilot). The subconscious mind is the reservoir of all that we have accepted as truth; it is our memory bank. By analogy, our conscious mind is the quarterback who calls the plays and makes decisions. Our subconscious mind represents the players who execute the plays (i.e., our behaviors).

Whenever we decide (with our conscious minds) to change our habits, we simply give new orders consciously to the subconscious mind. If these new orders (plays) are consistently put forth with clear diagrams and strong emotion over a period of time, they will be executed with precision.

Our habits are easy glimpses into our self-concepts. They reflect what we really think and feel about ourselves. Destructive habits are always indicative of low self-esteem. Conversely, good habits indicate healthy self-regard (or proper training).

So, how does one reprogram his or her subconscious mind in such a way that self-defeating habits can be interrupted or transformed into more positive, productive behaviors?

Let's study a concrete example: cigarette smoking. Those who smoke will readily admit that they have established stimuli-response patterns that usually dictate when they light up. So, the first step in breaking with bad habits is awareness. What usually triggers the undesirable behavior? Is the urge stronger at particular times? Are there anxiety-reducing alternatives available to the smoker?

It is also important to know that at the root of many negative behaviors, like smoking, is the operation of the "pleasure principle." In childhood, one of the ways that we learned was by seeking pleasure and avoiding pain. This pattern continues throughout our lives as well.

With cigarette smoking, what begins as an innocent and pleasure-filled act of association or adventure soon deteriorates into a destructive addiction. Each effort to wean oneself creates physical and emotional discomfort. To escape this displeasure, most will resort back to smoking (especially on their first effort to quit).

In our efforts to break with bad habits, it is crucial to understand that each newly acquired habit creates its own neural groove in our brains. If we would be willing to replace a bad habit with a more positive one for about three weeks, we could create a new groove that would cause new behavior patterns. Groovy, huh?

How do you begin? Project yourself ten years into the future. Ask yourself the question: By then, what toll will this bad habit have taken on me? Next, set a short-term, manageable goal to replace gradually a negative habit with a more positive one. Set modest goals but reward yourself generously at intervals for honest effort. If possible, engage the mutual support of someone else who is struggling against the same destructive habit. Seek professional help if you need it.

Lastly, use affirmations and creative visualization with the spoken word to build positive pictures of new habits. Unlike the lower animals, we are not limited by instinct. We are creative forces blessed with free will. We get to choose. Bad habits are the results of bad choices. Good habits are born of good choices. Self-love will guide you to a desire to form more good habits. Under the grounded control of good habits, your autopilot will take you to heights where only eagles fly. Flying high can also become a habit!

Questions

1. What are your good habits? How were they formed? List the various ways that you have benefited by having them to guide your daily activities.

2. Now, take ownership of your two or three worst habits. Try to pinpoint when they got a toehold in your life. What caused you to adopt them? What has been the cumulative cost of these self-defeating patterns?

3. Willpower may not be enough to break with bad habits. Imagination, if used properly, could potentially yield better results. How might you use your imagination to replace bad habits with good ones?

4. What role could rewarding oneself for desired behavior or enlisting the help of a friend or family member play in your efforts to extinguish bad habits?

ASSUMPTIONS BLUR OUR VISION

WHY DO WE ASSUME? WHY DO WE ACT AS IF OUR KNOWLEDGE base is loaded with correct information about other people and circumstances when, with a second, more honest look, we would have to admit that we really do not have all the facts? We assume other people's motives. We assume that we are limited. We assume that things will not work out. We assume that we can't when in reality, we can. We assume. We assume. We assume. Like the blind leading the blind, we follow our erroneous assumptions and then wonder why our moods are depressed, our love relationships are threatened, our children don't listen to us, our jobs don't fulfill us, and our lives don't excite us.

So I'll propose the question again. Why do we assume? Why do we draw premature conclusions before getting at least an adequate amount of factual information?

How many times have you judged another person wrongly only to later discover how far off your assessment was? I have done it on countless occasions. I'm learning to withhold my judgments of others and of myself.

I believe we rush to judge prematurely because it requires so little effort on our parts. The mental energy required to do the necessary fact-finding demands more of us than we are willing to give.

In addition, our unconscious minds are overloaded with negative beliefs born of past experiences. This part of our mind serves as an intricate tape-recording device. When we encounter an individual or situation even remotely resembling what is presently in front of us, we flip on the judgment switch and begin cruising on automatic pilot.

Another's words or the possibility that a particular situation is about to occur is linked with similar occurrences from the past and our conscious minds make the decision to lump the present and the past into one broad, easily-defined category.

For example, maybe when you were ten years old, you were asked to recite a poem for an assembly of the entire school. You had memorized it to perfection, or so you thought. Everyone at home had heard you deliver the poem with sheer glibness. Arriving at school that fateful morning, however, you felt butterflies in your stomach but felt that you had the necessary confidence to meet your pending challenge.

Then, fiasco! As the mistress of ceremony called your name, you immediately jumped to your feet but noticed your legs felt less stable than usual. In fact, you were convinced that they were going to collapse from the enormous weight of your ninety-eight-pound body.

Those harmless, early morning butterflies had now been transformed into aggressive predators mercilessly eating up the lining of your stomach. To exacerbate an already aggravated dilemma, you became aware that you were perspiring profusely. And your mouth—the mouth that you would so desperately need to speak with—suddenly became drier than an Arizona desert. If only water would run in the right places at desperate times like these, you thought to yourself.

After you approached the microphone and surveyed the packed auditorium, your feedback loop was overloaded with the self-conscious reality that hundreds of eyes were now all staring at you. The podium under your feet felt like it was turning into quicksand.

Panic. Hyperventilation. Then, deciding to rescue yourself from further torture, you finally spoke with parched tongue: "I can't do it. Sorry." With that uttered confession and very public humiliation, you went back to your seat and silently wished that the whole ordeal was only a bad dream. You vowed to yourself that you would never speak before an audience again.

You may possibly go through your whole life assuming that each occasion where you would be called to speak in public would be equally disastrous. If you allow your unchallenged assumptions to guide you, they could lead you to a life of painful limitations. *The past need not be prologue.* New possibilities and new beginnings abound. That is what makes life so interesting. We can change. We can overcome the nightmares of the past by redirecting our energies, by taking everything one step further, and by consciously challenging the limiting power of our assumptions.

One great mind once wrote: "Understanding is vertical and infinite." When we challenge our initial perceptions, when we withhold our premature conclusions, and when we question our safe and easy assumptions, we expand our scopes. We broaden the pictures that reality presents to us. We see more. We heighten our awareness. *We live more!*

Falling prey to easy conclusions from assumptions is indeed human. But daily challenging what we think we know about ourselves and others helps us to enjoy at least a glimpse of the divine.

Questions

1. Can we agree that assuming requires less effort than deferring judgment? If this conclusion is based on sound reasoning, the question that should be raised in context is this: what stimulus will be needed to prod us to put forth the added effort required to withhold our premature judgments of other people or situations?

2. Can you think of past incidents where assuming got you into hot water?

3. Assumptions are the culprits in the prejudging of other people, and they lurk behind all negative stereotypes. How have you personally been injured by other people's assumptions of who you are and what you are capable of doing?

4. What is the best way to overcome the lingering effects of the past fiascoes of your life?

5. How should you explain to a five year old the cost of assuming before one has diligently gathered the facts?

An Improved Attitude
The Choice is Yours

SO HOW WILL THE CURRENT YEAR BE FUNDAMENTALLY different from previous years? What is the one thing that *you can control* that will make the next year less stressful, more productive, and filled with more inner peace?

The answer is unequivocal: choose to nurture a positive mental attitude every day. Einstein was right: "It is not what we see, it is what we see with." Our attitudes will determine from one moment to the next how we "color" the facts presented by any situation. I'm not advocating a Pollyanna-like approach such as "positive thinking will solve all your problems." Some situations are dire or critical, and recognizing the graveness of a situation is an appropriate response.

Choosing, however, to view your circumstances from an elevated position (where you recognize the existence of a bigger picture and that time is not static) gives you an opportunity to see hidden blessings, even in a foreboding or dire situation. If we would seek in earnest the lessons of all apparent dilemmas, we would soon discover that life is usually trying to teach us a lesson that we are either too stubborn or too impatient to learn.

Our attitudes also shape our moods. This is important to know because our moods, in turn, determine whether we will tackle obstacles with enthusiasm or apathy. Of the two, you can guess which is more likely to get desired results. When you have a bad attitude, the whole world looks more dismal. You tend to focus on what is wrong with people, places, and things. With a bad attitude, you take your blessings for granted and complain incessantly about what is not right, what is not working, and how ungrateful or untrustworthy people are.

As a motivational trainer, Brian Tracy tells us that our attitudes are shaped by our expectations, which, in turn, are born of our overall belief system. Our belief system is rooted in our self-concept. Subconsciously, what we think and feel about ourselves shapes how we expect life will unfold for us. Although our self-concept began its formation in infancy, each of us has the power to reprogram the tape recordings buried deep within our psyches.

One of the most powerful ways to begin the ongoing process of reprogramming the mind and improving your mental attitude is to become aware of the nonstop conversation that goes on inside your head. Psychologists tell us that most of our self-talk is negative. If our goal for the current year is to improve our attitudes, we must listen more carefully to the discouraging, terrorizing, limiting, distrustful, and pessimistic things that *we tell ourselves!*

Next, go on the offensive. By analogy, most points are scored when a sports team is on the offensive rather than the defensive. So you can go on the offensive with what you choose to tell yourself about any situation. Ask yourself pointed questions. You'll marvel at the answers that will be distilled through the prism of a new attitude.

Am I socializing with individuals who lift my spirits or am I just trying to be a part of the "in crowd"? Do I think of ways to heap praise on family members and friends, or am I the perennial fault-finder? When doubts, worries, and fears run roughshod through my mind, creating one nightmarish mental video after another, do I, like a Hollywood movie director, shout "Cut!" or do I choose to let fear blind me of my many options and rob me of my serenity? Am I doing work that challenges me or am I just trying to pay the bills? Do I look forward to getting out of bed in the morning or do I dread facing a world fraught with danger and uncertainty?

It is all about our attitudes. We may not have the power to change everything that affects our lives. In many instances, the wise thing to do is to go with the flow or as believers would say, "let go and let God."

The bottom line is this: no matter what you are facing or will face this year, you will confront your concerns with more understanding, more resolve, and with a greater probability of successful outcome if you *choose to maintain a positive mental attitude!*

Questions

1. Honestly, on a scale of 1 to 10 (10 representing a very optimistic, resilient, and determined outlook on life and 1 representing a very defeatist, cynical, and pessimistic view of reality), where are you most of the time?

<————————————————————————————————>
1   5   10

2. Think of your favorite personalities—real or fictional—from your past. Which ones loomed largest as models to emulate? How would you characterize their overall attitudes toward life?

3. When someone has insulted you or attempted to undermine your intelligence, how have you allowed these transgressions to shape your attitudes in the past?

4. If attitude (moment-by-moment) is a simple matter of personal choice, why do we find it so easy to wallow in negative frames of mind or to suffocate in cesspool emotions?

5. Winners take personal responsibility for their predicaments. Losers look for someone to blame when things are not going well. Which are you most of the time? Which do you really want to be?

OUR MOODS COLOR OUR VIEW OF REALITY

LISTEN TO YOUR INTERNAL CONVERSATION. BECOME AWARE of the dialogue that goes on nonstop inside your own head. If you will pay close attention, you will be able to identify your mood.

Have you been focusing a lot of your thoughts on how you feel taken advantage of? Do you sometimes feel that your efforts are all in vain? That life does not hold much meaning for you?

Have you observed that when you are feeling unappreciated or unloved by your spouse, you are probably also finding fault with your job, your friendships, or your immediate prospects for improving your financial status?

It is nothing but a mood. Moods come and moods go. They are an inescapable feature of the human predicament. They color our view of reality. They determine whether we are satisfied or discontented with those important aspects of our lives. But our moods change so fast that a morning's glowing description of one's lovemate can by evening deteriorate into a litany of accusations and misunderstandings.

Here's the good news. We may not consciously place ourselves in a foul, depressing, aggravated mood but we can deliberately come out of it. Our moods are nothing more than barometers of our most persistent thoughts. If our heads are filled with negative, reactive, exaggerated, the-world-is-a-nightmare thoughts, our moods will reflect our self-defeating evaluations. If, on the other hand, we decide to ignore a barrage of hypercritical, judgmental, and anger-provoking thoughts and replace them with more truthful or hopeful ones, we will notice an elevation in our moods.

For example, in our very materialistic culture, no matter how much we acquire, we are never satisfied. Like hungry ghosts, we are haunted by an obsessive need to always want something other than what our present reality offers us. We tell ourselves that we will be happy when we get another job, lose ten pounds, find another lovemate, buy a new car, or move into a different house or apartment, on and on, ad nauseam.

If we would silence those noisy, troublesome thoughts inside our heads, we would soon discover (as one brilliant mind once wrote) that happy people are not those who get everything they want; rather, happy people are those who want what they have. You can always add something later. The secret, however, is to stop and focus genuinely with an attitude of gratitude on that which you already have. *An attitude of gratitude guarantees an elevation of your mood.*

Here's another proven method to lift your mood. Transcend yourself and focus on love: love of God, love of family, love of strangers, love of life, even love of your enemies. Focus on love. Consciously transmit it to others. Visualize yourself receiving the love and concern of others. Remember all emotions are rooted in either love or fear. When love dominates our thoughts and subsequently our feelings, our moods are buoyed effortlessly. We return to that state of emotional equilibrium called happiness. You will know when your mood has changed because you focus less on what's wrong in your life and more on what is right in it.

Some other obvious mood enhancers are: exercising, deep breathing, laughing, dancing, listening to music, praying, meditating, or just plain relaxing your mind and body.

The final and most powerful strategy for lifting oneself out of an ill-tempered mood is found in this simple admission: whatever I am going through at this moment in my relationships, with my finances, with my health, or with my attitude about life in general, I subconsciously created it. If I will take full responsibility for my situation and chart a more desirable course, I will begin to see the lessons in all my dilemmas and the solutions to all my problems.

Life has some wonderful moments to offer. But only those who ascend to loftier moods will be able to enjoy them.

Questions

1. For those who accept the popular slogan "Life is a bitch, then you die," any effort to sell them on the value of deliberate mood elevation tactics would, no doubt, be a waste of time. How might you mount an effective counteroffensive against chronically negative moods?

2. Why do you suppose that many people seem so comfortable being moody or cantankerous?

3. Have you ever noticed that you avoid certain people when you don't want to "spoil" a great mood? How might you avoid that spoiler disposition in yourself?

4. If it is true that our moods color our perception of our present reality, what color defines your most prevalent mood?

5. Think of someone you greatly admire. How would dining with them at a very elegant restaurant affect your mood?

6. Deliberately put yourself in a mood different than your present one. Notice how your thoughts and feelings are needed to create and maintain the altered mood state. What have you discovered about the power of choice in determining the mood that one enters or exits?

THE BLAME GAME IS LAME
Take Responsibility

OF ALL THE FALSE BELIEFS EMANATING FROM THE LOWER consciousness in each of us, none is more debilitating, more destructive, or more draining of our precious energies than the erroneous belief that someone or something other than ourselves is keeping us from actualizing our God-given potential. Others, at best or worst, are the catalysts. Our negative reactions to undesirable circumstances are created by our own misguided thoughts.

Whether it is a young supervisor claiming that he is producing far less than he is capable of producing because he was passed over for a promotion; the middle-age woman who regrets that her parents pushed her brother more to pursue higher education; the alcoholic blaming his addiction on the bad hand that life dealt him; or the teenager who accuses his peers of causing him to break into a neighborhood grocery store at midnight, individuals who play the blame game never quite seem to get it together.

If we are honest with ourselves, we will readily admit that at one time or another we all have found ourselves shirking from the responsibility for our role in creating some unfortunate predicament. At some point in our lives, all of us have played the blame game.

The problem with the blame game is this: even if others or situations overwhelmed us to the point that we felt urged to move in a direction that later proved to be too costly, we don't improve our conditions one iota by focusing blame for our present situation outside ourselves.

Reverend Jesse L. Jackson clearly stated this opinion: "I may not be responsible for getting knocked down. I am responsible for getting up." Blaming leaves us feeling down. Thoughts of being down cause us to lower our esteem as well as our expectations that we can bring it back up. Individuals as well as groups must always be ultimately held responsible for what they allow to happen to themselves. One great mind once wrote: "Oppression is not possible without at least the tacit approval of both oppressor and the oppressed."

A Taoist story from ancient China dramatizes the point of this essay:

> When Yen Ho was about to take up his duties as tutor to the heir of Ling, Duke of Wei, he went to Ch'u Po Yu for advice. "I have to deal," he said, "with a man of depraved and murderous disposition . . . How's one to deal with a man of this sort?"
>
> "I am glad," said Ch'u Po Yu, "that you asked this question . . . The first thing you must do is not to improve him, but to improve yourself."

From one moment to the next we refuse to improve ourselves and our situations by permitting much of what we experience. Even when unforeseen things (or events beyond our control) happen to us, we still occupy the driver's seat because we have the power to react and respond. If we react negatively, we give external events and other people power over us. If we respond positively (and the word *responsibility* literally means "the ability to respond"), we are able to harness our mental energies in such a way that the best possible result becomes a calculated option.

The blame game is also lame for another reason. If it becomes habitual, it clouds the future and limits our beliefs about what is really possible for our lives.

Even corporate America has identified a strategy to alter the rules of the blame game. Workers are encouraged not to ask who is to blame when something goes wrong. Instead, the individual confronting a malfunction in the delivery of goods or services is empowered to ask: "What can I do to help remedy the situation?"

So as you take an inventory of the assets and liabilities that constitute the ledger of your life, try not to waste time pointing the finger of blame; it will only leave you feeling knocked down. Instead, empower yourself by lending yourself a helping hand that always motivates you to want to get up and try again.

Questions

1. All of us have suffered at the hands of caprice, but much of our emotional pain is born of our refusal to accept some present reality that is facing us. How does taking responsibility for one's attitude improve an unfortunate situation—whether you created it or not?

2. The daily news bombards us with countless examples of man's inhumanity to man. How does one shield his or her psyche from these daily assaults against our peace of mind?

3. Ghalil Gibran, the great poet-philosopher, once stated: "The source of our greatest joy is also the source of our greatest pain." If you believe there is wisdom in his statement, how might you mitigate some of the pain that seems to come in your joy packages?

4. It is easier to focus on someone else's contribution to our unhappiness. Why do you suppose most of us find it so difficult to recognize the source of a lion's share of the responsibility for most of our misery?

5. The next time you find yourself suffering from protracted anger directed at someone, ask yourself how much of that anger could you be unconsciously directing at yourself?

6. Who do you blame for your good health, your food, your clothing, your home, or your happy times?

PROCRASTINATION
Why Do We Do It?

IT MAY BE IRONIC, BUT I PROCRASTINATED WRITING THIS essay more than any other in this series on the mind and motivation.

A plausible explanation for the postponement may well have been the number of times that my subconscious mind heard the word *procrastination*. Being the genius-servant that it is, the subconscious mind probably took my obsessing over an article that, at least temporarily, I seemed to have been incapable of writing as an order to *procrastinate*.

So, for a few weeks, I knew that I eventually had to take pen to paper and try to communicate with the reader on a topic that robs millions of people of their peace of mind. Most of us are not aware of why we procrastinate or the price that we pay for doing so.

Why do we procrastinate? I believe procrastination stems from a number of different reasons. The following is probably only a partial listing:

- we have not decided that we are going to undertake the task at hand;
- we have not chosen to make the task a priority;
- we honestly don't know how to get started;
- we're stuck in some comfort zone from which the beckoning task would stir us;
- we already have too much on our plates;
- we have not given ourselves a reason why the task is sufficiently important;
- we did not examine the effort that the task would require before agreeing with ourselves or others that we would perform it;
- we don't have a clear picture of the benefits of getting the task completed;
- we genuinely do not want to do the work necessary to complete the task.

H. L. Hunt once stated: "Decide what you want. Decide what you are willing to exchange for it. Establish your priorities."

It is all about choices. I had to give myself a good reason why I should choose to write an article on procrastination. The compelling reason that surfaced was this: I believe that procrastination not only robs millions of people of countless hours of peace of mind, but it also lowers our self-esteem, shakes our self-confidence, and postpones the achievement of goals or dreams that exist only in the murky recesses of our daily reveries.

A remarkable person once wrote, "In the end we either have excuses or experiences; reasons or results; buts or brilliance." How insightful.

If we would think through our choices, guard against the human proclivity for wasting our precious moments, and accept only those tasks that we sincerely believe ought to be done and done in a timely fashion, we will find that hours of restless procrastination will be replaced with a life filled with more inner peace.

Whether or not the task at hand is job-related, school-related, or family-related and looks too big to tackle, apply the wisdom of the great thinker who reminded us: "It's hard by the yard but it's a cinch by the inch." Break the work down into manageable pieces. The greatest challenge is getting started. The German poet Goethe advised in one of his couplets: "If you can do a thing or think you can, begin it; boldness has genius and magic in it."

It is important, however, to think through your strategy. It is also wise to take your own counsel when you feel that your knowledge base is inadequate to commence with your project. Most of the time, procrastination is just a bad habit, causing us to act contrary to our own best interests. Procrastination is subtle, but its impact on our lives, careers, and overall sense of well-being can be absolutely devastating.

In addition, demonstrating inactivity where activity is required, taking the path of least resistance, and having to rush to get a job done at the last minute are all behavior patterns of losers. Winners know that decisiveness and prompt action are the routes taken to attain great achievements. They also know that when we do what we need to do at the right time, we will later be able to do what we really want to do when we really want to do it.

It's about winning in a struggle with self in a lifelong battle that none of us should want to lose.

So, are there times when inactivity is appropriate? Absolutely. Rest and relaxation are critical in the formula for successful living. Patiently awaiting the harvests from one's labors is often the approach taken by the wise. A heightened sense of self will help you to determine when your inactivity is bona fide procrastination.

Lastly, confront procrastination at its incipiency. Nip it in the bud. Decide as soon as possible that you will not allow an unconscious urge to sabotage you. If you have decided that a pending task is important, tackle at least some part of it *today,* or even *now* if possible!

I'll leave you with a bit of wisdom that summarizes the message of this section with sheer elegance:

Let us, then, be up and doing,
With a heart for any fate;
Still achieving, still pursuing,
Learn to labor and to wait.
—Henry Wadsworth Longfellow
A Psalm of Life

Questions

1. Please close the book for a few minutes. Close your eyes. Conjure up in your mind the last two or three tasks that you found yourself putting off or avoiding. Think of the reasons why you have postponed these activities. Upon a second glance, are these really the reasons that you procrastinated?

2. What have you noticed about a sense of urgency to get things done in the people who seem to take on more than their share of responsibilities at home, work, or in the community?

3. Place yourself in the emergency room in dire need of medical care. The admitting clerk has gratuitously forewarned you that the doctor you so desperately want to see "always takes his time." How might the habit of procrastination eventually prove to be very costly?

4. You may be thinking: "Sometimes I am just lazy or unmotivated. It is human to seek comfort. Why not procrastinate sometimes just because it feels good not to do something that demands my energy." What is faulty about this line of reasoning?

5. Make up your own slogan to help overcome the habit of procrastination. Commit it to memory. After a couple of weeks, observe if your attitude about putting things off has begun to change for the better.

SELF-ACCEPTANCE
AND SELF-LOVE
*The Foundations for Good
Human Relations*

PERFECTION IN THIS LIFE IS NOT AN ATTAINABLE GOAL; however, living a fulfilled life with much contentment or peace of mind is attainable. Therefore, why agonize over the former objective when you can enjoy the latter? Why is it so important that we accept ourselves as we are and learn to really love—not merely tolerate—ourselves?

First, self-acceptance. Walter Cronkite, the celebrated former news anchor, would conclude his daily chronicles of newsworthy events with an emphatic "And that's the way it is." To paraphrase Cronkite, I would like to challenge you to take an honest look at yourself, with all your strengths, weaknesses, good judgments, fiascoes, kind gestures, and outbursts of anger, and simply state: "And this is the way I am." Accept it. You may not be perfect but *you are perfectly you!* One of six billion inhabitants on this small planet rotating in infinite space, you are unique in all creation.

Seeing yourself—flaws and all—and telling yourself that you accept who and what you are is mentally healthy and an important ingredient in your search for a formula for happiness. Accepting yourself is not tantamount to condoning undesirable behavior, nor is acceptance necessarily approving. Acceptance is acknowledging the reality of who you are at this point in your personal development.

Why is self-acceptance so important? It is important because you get to declare a truce with yourself. Your inner walls of resistance come down. All of that wasted psychic energy can now be rechanneled for more positive thinking, more constructive feeling, and more fulfilled living.

Some of the harshest judgments that we pass, we heap upon ourselves: "I should have done this" or "I should have done that"; "How could I have been so stupid?"; or "I can never forgive myself for what I did." If we start to listen to that nonstop conversation that goes on inside our heads, we become painfully aware that we are not accepting the reality of the human condition. Once we accept ourselves, forgive ourselves, and shift our focus towards what it is we want to accomplish with our lives, guilt, shame, low esteem, and a sense that somehow we just do not measure up to some unreachable ideal will be replaced with a newfound inner peace.

In addition, accepting ourselves as we are is a necessary predicate for accepting others as they are. The benefits of this new awareness can be incalculable.

We desperately want to be accepted as we are. Much of our self-worth and sense of belonging are inextricably intertwined with the degree of acceptance that we receive from others—especially our significant others.

Acceptance of ourselves and others is a prelude to more harmonious human relations.

Now, what about self-love? A neo-Freudian, Dr. Erich Fromm once wrote: "Love is the active concern for the growth and development of the beloved." Apply this definition to the way you feel about and ultimately treat yourself.

By testing how much you really do love yourself (not to be confused with degrees of narcissism), how would you answer the following questions:

1. Do you find time everyday to do something—large or small—that pleases you?

2. Do you allow others to place demands on your energy and resources when you would rather say no?

3. Do you forgive yourself for the mistakes that you make?

4. Do you allow anger to fester like a sore inside you or to erupt like a volcano? (Note: our most intense angry feelings for others—especially if the anger is prolonged—is usually anger directed at ourselves. Please be forewarned that protracted, intense forms of anger have been associated with heart attacks, ulcers, and other threatening medical conditions.)

5. Do you actively pursue your greatest interests?

6. Do you allow family members or friends to make continuous comments about you which leave you feeling anxious, insecure, intimidated, overwhelmed, or resentful?

7. Do you allow yourself to express your true feelings with individuals or within a group, or do you feel that you must "go along to get along?"

8. Do you take good care of your body or is it treated like a dumping ground for toxic waste?

9. What do you tell yourself about your abilities and what you are entitled to receive from life?

10. How long do you endure unpleasant situations and people before you decide to choose a better place or more enjoyable space?

11. Typically, during the course of a day, how often do you laugh?

Like self-acceptance, self-love is the starting point for living life at its best. To use the analogy of concentric circles—like those seen when you toss a pebble into a lake—our deepest feelings for ourselves radiate out to others. In karmic fashion, the acceptance and love of others is sent back to us, oftentimes not in ripples, but in tidal waves.

Become aware of whether or not you routinely accept and love yourself. Consciously listen to your own thoughts about yourself. If you choose a more positive approach with yourself, this old troubled world will not only no longer get you down, but you will soon discover that you have created your own light. Thus, when combined with the light of others like yourself, you will be able to help stamp out much of the darkness that characterizes human relations on our planet today.

Questions

1. What aspect of your personality do you like best? With what aspect are you least satisfied?

2. From childhood, we learned to value or not value ourselves based on whether or not we were affirmed (accepted) by others. How might you depend less on the opinion of others and more on yourself for validation?

3. To varying degrees, there appears to be a critic inside ourselves incessantly reminding us of our imperfections. Consciously construct a dialogue with the critic within, but insist that only true statements about who you really are will be accepted as valid.

4. If you have ever tried to stop smoking cigarettes, lose weight, or force more discipline on yourself, you have known how much it hurts to be unaccepting of yourself. Why do you suppose that beating up on yourself rarely gets the results which you ultimately seek?

5. Children intuitively know they cannot be perfect. How might you consult the child within to relearn how to be at peace—and even enjoy—some of your shortcomings?

6. Imagine how you would feel at the end of a day during which all of your conscious thoughts and feelings for yourself were guided by self-love.

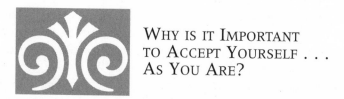

WHY IS IT IMPORTANT
TO ACCEPT YOURSELF . . .
AS YOU ARE?

YOU ARE NEVER THE PERSON YOU ARE BECOMING. THAT IDEAL, floating somewhere in a remote future, is never enjoyed in the only time period that any of us really has—the present. Much of our internal conflict is born of trying to avoid one of the most dreadful experiences known to our species: being socially ostracized. We all suppress many of our creative impulses when we attempt to lose our identity in the mass glob of conformity.

It's okay to be who you are right now. You may never be perfect but you will always be perfectly you.

In an organized society, there are obviously instances when conformity to certain standards of behavior minimizes harm to the sensibilities of others. Courteous, civil behavior promotes social harmony, goodwill, and maybe even progress. But where should we draw the line? This line that separates the authentic self from societal pressures must be continuously redefined to prevent intrusive norms from militating against an individual's right to be.

In the world of motivation or in the business of developing human potential, individuals are encouraged to seek their purpose. Purpose is our life's calling. It is our microcosm. It is our piece of the puzzle of creation. It is our divinely assigned role on the stage of life.

Many have gone to the precipice, suffering unmitigated internal conflict from trying to balance their need to be, with other people's desires to force uniformity. Face it: we are all different. Six billion of us occupy this relatively small space called earth. It is obvious that there does exist a need for a social contract. There are certain norms that enhance the quality of social interaction, civility, and a desired predictability of human behavior. But each of us is unique. A part of that uniqueness must be allowed if the grand design of creation is to unfold as it should.

It takes courage to be oneself. Freud referred to much of the time that he spent alone as "splendid isolation." Oftentimes, solitude is the only way to find oneself in a world that celebrates banality and stifles creative self-expression.

A wise aunt advised me in my youth: "Don't follow the crowd; lead it." In my immaturity and innocence, I uncritically accepted her statement to represent a higher intelligence. Today, with the passing of years, her exhortation rings with power and clarity. If you are a creation of the mob's mind, you allow yourself to be relegated to an inferior position, ordained by unthinking men and women, rather than to be guided by a higher calling that beckons you to become who you were destined to be . . . *a marvel to the world!*

We are social beings. We need each other's love, sometimes even each other's acceptance, for a sense of well-being. But we also never need to sacrifice who we really are and what we really believe for the pseudo-comfort of others' approval. As one great mind so aptly stated it, we should not "Worship the god of other people's opinions." Psychologists tell us that most people do not approve of themselves most of the time. Why, then, should we overvalue their approvals of us? Most people have not "walked a mile in our shoes," so how can they possibly understand what we ought to do or be?

If I lose weight, great. If I stop smoking, marvelous. If I join the health club and get into a regimen, wonderful. If I save money, smart. If I control my temper, prudent. If I give to worthwhile causes, noble. But I do not have to do any of the above in order to accept and love myself as I find myself at this present moment.

Try it. After reading this essay, immediately begin practicing the art of self-acceptance. Silence that irritating inner voice that keeps pushing the bar higher and higher before you can feel all-right about yourself. It finally dawned on me that ideals are our striving targets. Oftentimes, we miss the mark. In spite of this, we should celebrate our efforts rather than ridicule ourselves for undesired results.

Struggle to improve? Yes. Strive to develop your potential? Absolutely. Want to give your best? Why not? But waiting for the outcome before accepting yourself—no way!

Questions

1. What does the statement "You may never be perfect but you are perfectly you" mean?

2. Declare a truce with yourself. For one hour refuse to entertain any thought or feeling that causes you to reject yourself.

3. Why does it take courage to be who you are?

4. Some great mind said, "Be careful what word you allow to follow 'I am _____.'" Think of a few occasions recently where you have been your own worst critic. How did it leave you feeling about yourself?

5. How might you examine your life in order to enhance its quality without denigrating yourself?

PART II

"All our fears grow out of a core fear of loss: loss of control, love, esteem or health."

—JAMES J. MAPES
QUANTUM LEAP THINKING

FEAR
Illuminate to Dissipate

LET'S PLACE THE SUBJECT OF FEAR UNDER THE MICROSCOPE. Yes, we are going to get scientific in our approach to understanding this notorious villain and sometimes friend.

So what is fear? Fear is only an emotion. Fear often serves a positive purpose in our struggle for survival. It is the offspring of the ancient fight-or-flight syndrome. Fear can save our lives. Fear can give us added energy. Fear can heighten our awareness in the face of real danger or a demanding challenge.

If we understand the proper use of fear, it is our friend. However, the vast majority of our fears are irrational and unhealthy. They fit in the category of what one writer calls: "**F**alse **E**vidence **A**ppearing **R**eal." Irrational fear is at the root of all negative emotions. Yet, it has no more power over us than we can give it.

When we are worrying, the culprit is fear. When we are frustrated, the culprit is fear. When we are afraid to be ourselves, the culprit is fear. When we are angry, the culprit is fear. When we are anxious about the future, the culprit is always fear.

Our insecurities are born of our fears. The primary reason why most people live out their lives "in quiet desperation" is because of this psychic intruder. *Fear can paralyze us. It stops us in our tracks. It causes us to shrink from some of life's greatest challenges.*

Through countless acts of mental and emotional sabotage, irrational fears infiltrate our minds and take control of our powerful imaginations. Fear distorts reality's clear pictures by first creating disturbing images on our inner screens.

The reason fear is able to get a foothold inside our heads remains our lack of awareness. The most important thing that we can do to counter fear's impact is to become aware of its scary presence. But do not resist fear. It is only a shadow. There is nothing to fight. The only thing necessary to prove how powerless our irrational fears are is to refuse to react to them.

Refuse to react to fear? How is that taking control of my fears? You do not take control of fears; you simply observe them. You illuminate to dissipate. The best weapon in your arsenal against fear is awareness. You must get a greater understanding of where the fear is coming from.

If you refuse to "energize" your fears by withholding any emotional response to them over a period of time, they will eventually evaporate into thin air. Why? Because they are not real!

Think about it. There are things that you want to do with your life right now and yet, the great trickster (fear) is holding you back, causing unnecessary pain. Not pursuing our highest calling for personal fulfillment is painful. Not fully exploring this wonderful experience called life is painful. Worrying about what others think of us is painful. What lurks at the core of all this pain? You got it—fear.

Look back over your life. Examine all the times that you desperately wanted to break out of your comfort zone and try something different, or that you envied someone else for breaking free of fear's stranglehold. As you look back, think of the inspiring words of President Franklin D. Roosevelt, who lifted a dispirited nation with his famous words: "So let me assert my firm belief that the only thing we have to fear is fear itself—nameless, unreasoning, unjustified terror which paralyzes needed efforts to convert retreat into advance."

If you will move from fear's shadowy cave of doubt and despair into the encouraging light of understanding, you will realize that there really is nothing to fear but fear itself.

When fear acts as a friend, warning you against real danger or energizing you to face real challenges, you should acknowledge its beneficial role. But when fear tries to get you to believe that you are defeated, you should, with keen awareness, shine the light of understanding on it. This will be sufficient to send it scurrying back "onto the heap of its native nothingness." And you will emerge victorious!

Questions

1. It has been said that fear is at the root of all negative emotions. Can you see why this statement might be valid?

2. James Mapes concluded in his book, *Quantum Leap Thinking,* that fear is all about losing something. What are you most afraid to

lose? How might you characterize that loss that you fear most? If it is death that you fear most, ask yourself, other than pain and suffering, what is it about death that creates so much fear?

3. When has fear acted as your friend or ally?

4. List three examples of irrational fears. How might shining the light of understanding help you to dissipate your irrational fears?

5. What fears from childhood do you still harbor? What might your adult awareness tell the child within in order to bring forth tranquility in the face of fear?

6. What is your greatest fear today? How do you suppose you will feel about this fear if you understood why you were so afraid?

 BEYOND FEAR'S FENCE . . .

BEYOND FEAR'S FENCE AWAITS FAITH'S FORTUNE. THIS IS ONE of the greatest lessons that life has taught me. Each time that I confronted my fears (dating back to the first grade at age six), I later discovered that beyond fear's powerful grip, something really nice awaited me.

The business of motivation has taken me down many avenues, across much terrain, and brought me face-to-face with many dreaded fears: those of failure, rejection, inadequacy, and alienation. Oftentimes, my imagination would race ahead with foreboding outcomes that would never materialize. Fear was trying to discourage me.

Our imaginations are the theaters of our subconscious minds. We act out our strongest held beliefs that reside beneath the surface of our conscious awareness. The scary scenes produced by fear are manifestations of what we really believe in our subconscious minds. Refusing to bow to fear's limiting potential causes the subconscious mind to switch its programming to more pleasant possibilities.

When each of us decides to leave our comfort zones and break away from habitual patterns of thinking and doing, we often experience in our bodies a certain discomfort. We also become aware of a certain psychological uneasiness. Because human beings tend to approach pleasure and avoid pain (in any form), we tend to shy away from fear-provoking experiences and the pain that we associate with them.

For example, you may have told yourself that your present job, spouse or significant other, group of friends, or financial status is not what you want. You are beginning to experience *ennui* (boredom) too often. You have noticed that your life is lacking a certain zest. You rarely feel upbeat about anything. Past pleasures have become blasé. You know that it is time to make a few life-altering changes.

> *"Fear only holds power over you when it goes unacknowledged."*
>
> —JAMES J. MAPES
> *Quantum Leap Thinking*

Once you reach this point on the path of life's journey, you are forced to make a decision. Will you proceed further along this uneventful and enervating course, where your appetite for nearly everything has become dulled? Or will you take the time to closely examine what is really going on inside you? A few days of quiet introspection will probably reveal a truth that lies right beneath the surface of your awareness: you are being called to confront your fears. You are being summoned by a higher command to come out of the comfort zone (i.e., your daily rut). You are being challenged to leap over fear's fence to enjoy the promise of an abundant life.

Some great mind has insightfully stated that the only constant in life is change. As we grow, our bodies change. As we mature, our behavior changes. In addition, as we study life's lessons, our perceptions change. But change is difficult because it requires saying good-bye to familiar people, places, and patterns. Change means letting go. Change means facing the unknown. Change is about risk and insecurity. But change is inevitable. Hence, those who resist change do so at their own peril.

Irrational fear is usually an indication that we are resisting change. We shrink; we recoil; we seek to hide in the illusion of permanence. We cling to the past because of a fear of facing the future, inadvertently abandoning the richness found only in the courageous present.

Like so many other ironies found in human existence, those who most often seek comfort in past patterns usually end up suffering the most discomfort when they focus on future predicaments.

The challenge for each of us is simply to let go. Let go of the false beliefs that fear notoriously nourishes. Let go of a paradigm that stifles growth and rewards the status quo. Let go of those thoughts that lure you into thinking that the unknown is overwhelmingly fraught with danger or frightful outcomes. Like the young child trying to ride a bicycle for the first time or taking that first plunge into a swimming pool, view yourself confronting your fears and moving beyond them.

When we care enough for ourselves to become devoted stewards of our own development; when we love ourselves enough to take a risk on ourselves; and when we courageously decide to stretch for life's wonderful possibilities instead of seeking a suffocating certainty, we will inevitably rejoice in the incontrovertible truth that *beyond fear's fence awaits faith's fortune.*

Questions

1. What great blessings possibly await you on the other side of fear's fence?

2. What is the connection between fear and low self-esteem?

3. If courage is not the absence of fear, what is courage?

4. Many people are afraid to face the countless changes that life will force them to face. How might you attain harmony with the inevitable changes of life?

5. When is fear only an illusion?

6. How might you overcome your fear of failure?

DESIRE IS STRONGER
THAN FEAR

HOW HAS FEAR HELD YOU BACK? HAVE YOU CONTEMPLATED going into business for yourself but continued to postpone the idea for fear of leaving the "secure" paycheck? Have you found yourself clinging to someone in a love relationship that is defined by persistent frustration, anger, deceit, and a disquieting notion that it's going nowhere? Or maybe you are plagued by one of the many phobias that create minefields full of fearful traps all over your field of dreams?

At first glance, it would appear that the old phantom fear is unstoppable in its fiendish goal to prevent each of us from developing our God-given potential.

Fear will invade the private world of your innermost thoughts and stifle your would-be-plans for growth, more fulfillment, greater achievement, a sincere desire to give something of value to others, or just enjoying a sense of well-being that tells you that everything will work out fine. Unchallenged, fear can and does wreak havoc on our lives. It relishes its headlock on our minds, suffocating the brain's activity and dissipating our creative energies.

So what must you do to lessen fear, or better yet, to drive a stake through its life-sucking heart? The answer is rather simple in terms of common sense but not common practice: *focus more energy on desire.*

Desire is stronger than fear. It is absolutely true that a burning passion for something will give you the added fuel to drive right through the illusionary wall created by fear. But weak, equivocating desire will not suffice. The type of desire to which I refer must be deeply rooted and energized by compelling reasons. *You must know why you want what you want!*

For example, I know a woman who has two sons who are attending colleges in other states. She once stated emphatically that she would never fly: "Airplanes terrify me." Her subconscious mind had so entangled all air travel with fiery crashes that she equated all plane rides with certain death. Case closed. Right? Maybe not.

One Monday morning she received a call that one of her sons had been injured in an serious automobile accident. She was told that he was in the hospital and in critical condition. Over the telephone the chief of surgery advised this woman that her son might not make it through the night.

Without giving it a second thought, she decided that she had to travel the necessary one thousand miles in the quickest way possible— by airplane. Within seconds of hanging up the telephone receiver, the mother was packing to catch the next flight to Boston, Massachusetts.

During the hour between packing and arriving at the airport, the fear of flying had no power over her. Her attention was strongly focused on her desire to see her son alive, maybe for the last time. Her desire proved to be much stronger and more motivational than her fear.

If, however, exigent circumstances do not create an intensity of desire for you, you may have to manufacture your own compelling reasons to conquer fear. But only by defeating fear are any of us able to move to the exciting realm of what is really possible for our lives. The good news is that it is always within our power to do so.

Desire and fear are both strong emotions. But desire causes us to shift our focus. Desire silences the dreaded conversations within our heads, instead replacing them with an inner dialogue that creates pictures of a positive outcome and forces the darker, more ominous scenes to fade to the background.

So the next time you become aware that fear has you in its grip, break its stranglehold by consciously shifting your thoughts to reasons why you must get beyond the fear. Focus with intensity. Use the awesome power of your imagination to "see," in vivid colors, the object of your desire.

This is why the process of setting goals is most effective when we begin with the end result in mind. The end result allows us to enjoy a preview of the desired outcome.

Even if you already had this tidbit of wisdom safely tucked away in your mental organizer, take a few minutes to really think about how—if applied in everyday living—this valuable insight could drive you forward while putting your fear in reverse gear.

Questions

1. What do you desire most from life? How has fear threatened to undermine the joy or pleasure that your desires bring you?

2. Use a technique called "paradoxical intention" and convince yourself that you can be content even if you were denied your greatest pleasure.

3. In Buddhist meditation, practitioners are warned of the inevitable pain that follows becoming too attached to anything. How might you use this wisdom to pursue the desires of your heart without becoming neurotically attached?

4. Possibly, the reason that desire creates the motivation to overcome fear is that when we desire something good or we desire someone, we are tapping into that positive energy flow called love. How might you use the energies of love to overcome your greatest fears?

5. Close your eyes. Imagine that someone you love greatly is entrapped in a medieval castle. You have only a few hours to save the life of your loved one. The castle, in true storybook fashion, is surrounded by a moat full of hungry crocodiles and vicious sharks. As you construct a strategy for the rescue of your loved one, notice how your mind shifts its energies to give the advantage to that which you desire rather than that which you fear.

FAITH
Indispensable Ingredient
of Success

NO ONE ACCOMPLISHES GREATNESS, NO ONE LIVES A triumphant life, and no one does anything of historical significance without faith. Yet, holding onto one's faith is not easy. It takes tremendous effort to move into the darkness of uncertainty, hoping in spite of discouraging appearances that the day hoped for will come.

From our sometimes shaky belief in the Almighty to our troublesome concerns about our lovemates, job stability, health, or the future, many of us struggle daily to hold onto the belief that our efforts are not in vain.

Faith, if fostered, will get you wherever you are trying to go. Faith puts us in touch with the genius of our subconscious minds and the power of the Universal Mind of God.

Faith is the great connector between our present predicament and of things hoped for in the future. Faith (with the help of modern medicine) shrinks cancerous tumors, lifts determined souls out of poverty, confers college degrees, fires the entrepreneurial spirit, stands and defeats the odds, crushes doubt's destructive defenses, frees the mind of countless worries, and calls us back into battles that we once thought we would never reenter.

Faith is the bomb. It gives courage its armor and love its endurance.

Faith lifts purpose to a place of adoration and weakens the allure of despair. Faith beckons us onward and upward to answer the call of noble sacrifice and genuine contribution to making this a better world for ourselves and others.

Maintaining faith, however, is not easy. Faith is fed only by choices deeply rooted in character; our choices emanate from our core values. Who we are and what we value determine the quality of our faith.

If we nurture a strength of spirit born of disciplined effort and conscious choice, we can build a solid foundation for an enduring faith. How we react to failure, pain, and disappointment determines whether or not we make ourselves more capable of sustaining a fortified faith "in things unseen."

Faith begets more faith. The more we see the fruits of our faith the stronger it becomes.

Our minds are mental magnets. We attract that which we believe will happen. Our beliefs help us to create the lives that we live. Steadfastly believing our dreams will materialize if we refuse to give over to doubt, refusing to give in to weak effort, and refusing to give up on tomorrow's possibilities lead inevitably to the rewards that faith can bestow.

Faith took *Ebony* magazine's John Johnson from poverty to an empire. Faith took Dr. Martin Luther King Jr. from local preacher to worldwide personality. Faith took Booker T. Washington's idea for aiding rejected sharecroppers from insight to institution. Faith caused Marva Collins, Chicago's educator extraordinaire, to turn failing children into fantastic children.

Faith will work for you, too. Decide what is most important to you. In the hierarchy of your priorities, what ranks as number one? What really drives you? What causes you to periodically move out of your comfort zone? What is your purpose, your reason for living?

> *"Faith is the substance of things hoped for, the evidence of things not seen."*
>
> —Hebrews 11:1

After you have determined what is truly important, you have set the stage for bringing some new reality into being. Whatever it is that you will create, faith will act as your "bridge over troubled water." How stable that bridge will be is determined by the mental toughness of the builder. Please believe that weak faith is always a prelude to collapse.

So commit yourself to a daily process of building stronger faith. As you move further into the realm of the unknown, you will have cause to celebrate. From deep within, your sweet conviction will echo with the reassurance that you are traveling with "the substance of things hoped for" and buttressed by "the evidence of things not seen."

Questions

1. Incessant worrying and persistent doubting are examples of strong faith. They represent faith that something bad will happen. What do you put your faith in everyday?

2. Wayne Dyer wrote a book entitled *You See It When You Believe It.* Apply this wisdom to create the "evidence of things not seen."

3. Most of us believe only what we see. How does this approach to faith differ from the mental processes used by great inventors and celebrated thinkers?

4. In Holy Scripture, we are told: "Nothing shall be impossible unto you." Looking over your lifetime of experiences, have you found this statement to be true? What mindset always creates the seemingly miraculous?

5. Give yourself an example of how applied faith got you through one of life's raging storms.

 Live in the Present

AS OUR SOCIETY ENTERED THE 1950s, MORE BOOKS AND articles were being published to herald the dawning of the "Age of Anxiety." Anxiety is disquietude. It is apprehensiveness. It is also about the future, the outcome, and the unknown. Guilt is dreadful concern about the past; anxiety is a dreadful preoccupation with the future.

Here's the good news. The vast majority of things that we are anxious about never come to pass. It has been estimated that 96 percent of our worries are concerned with events or situations that never occur. The angst that leaves us feeling so unsettled, so perturbed—like many other negative, punishing feelings—is born of false thinking and alarmist visualizing.

Unfortunately, most of us have gotten into a habit of feeling anxious. But our flights into an abyss of foreboding thoughts and feelings are not solo ones. We get an ample amount of help from our very negative environments. The daily media sources— television, radio, and newspapers—feed listening and reading audiences large doses of disturbing, distorted, and dishonest depictions of our world.

Rather than giving balanced accounts of the events of the day, major news organizations have become pandering peddlers of people's pain. Wallowing in decadence, death, and depravity, much of today's news appeals to and nurtures the darker side of human nature. We get affected because our thoughts and feelings are not generated in a vacuum. We think, feel, and act in tandem with the world around us.

The human spirit naturally struggles against the negative. The human spirit moves outward to embrace life and upward to enhance it. To buffer itself from the ugly realities that sometimes will bombard it, the spirit—working through the human imagination—will begin to dream or fantasize by seeking something that is more beautiful, more uplifting, and more gratifying than a present reality which appears uninviting at best, and gloomy at worst.

So we dream. We dream of a time in the future where financial security replaces burdensome financial obligations. We dream of a day when we are surrounded by a type of love resembling William Shakespeare's definition in his well-known sonnet: "That looks on tempest and is never shaken . . . that bears it out even until the edge of doom . . ." We fantasize about a time when our bodies will look as if we have reversed evolution's march and regained our youthful appeal.

We dream of a time when we can just relax and enjoy the small sweet things that once made life so enchanting. We yearn for a future reality in which stress is under control and health has been restored. We also hope that one day we will be able to control our tempers, be more forgiving of others, think before we speak, cease gossiping, and overcome our worst addictions. It seems that all of our joys, our peace of mind, and the real fun of living are always somewhere in the distant future. Even as we feel so much anxiety about what might be, we also steadfastly hold on to the belief that if there is any real happiness for us, it will be found in tomorrow. We are focusing on the future at the expense of the present!

Now, for the unbridled truth: the only happiness that any of us will ever know, can only be known in the present. We are never in the future. The future is an artificial construct. We have only the ever-present present. What joy there is must be found in the present moment, the miraculous NOW!

Becoming increasingly popular, Buddhist meditation helps practicing individuals get totally focused in the present. Its goal is mindfulness, which causes the practitioner to suspend all mental chatter, cease all worries, and withhold all judgments. The meditating individual is called inward. Deep breathing and recitations of the chosen mantra aid the process. But the goal is to get the individual to become more aware of being in the present.

When we consciously force our thoughts to focus on the present moment, our perception of reality changes. If we will collaborate with what life is revealed by allowing ourselves to get in life's flow, we would begin to live in the here and now. Then we would come to realize that dreaming and planning, as important as they may be, are supporting actors and actresses at best. The starring role—from the beginning of the show until the grand finale—is always assigned to the life that we are living in the present moment.

Though we may not be aware of it, the present moment has all the joy, peace, and love that any future moment could ever have. All we have to do is open our eyes to see.

Questions

1. Why is it that human beings spend so little time enjoying the golden moment (the here and now)?

2. Twenty or thirty years from today, someone will refer to the end of the twentieth century and the beginning of the next as the "good ol' days." Why do we look upon the past with nostalgia rather than enjoying today (which will be the past tomorrow)?

3. What happened in your past that you cannot forgive yourself for? What will it take for you to let go of the past and start living in the present?

4. Someone once wrote: "The past is over; no one knows what the future will hold. All we have is the gift of now. That is why we call it 'the present.'" What gifts of the present are you taking for granted?

5. Get completely still. Calm down. Take ten deep breaths; inhale and exhale slowly. Close your eyes. Silence your "inner chatter." Now, answer this question with as much honesty as you can muster: "What's really so bad about my life right now?"

 HAPPINESS

GUY FINLEY'S BOOK SAYS IT ALL. IF WE WOULD TRULY "WANT what life wants," we would cease with our desultory penchant of expecting everything and everybody to conform to our ideas about what ought to be.

It appears that happiness is an attainable goal. But as Finley's book so insightfully reminds us, we must be willing to let go of "a self that thinks clinging to wreckage is the same as being rescued."

Finley explains the dichotomy between who we mistakenly think we are versus who we really are. He exposes a false self that keeps us imprisoned by our slavish reactions to negative emotions (i.e., fear, anxiety, worry, resentment, jealousy, insecurity, etc.). If we refuse to energize these destructive emotions, they will subside. He talks about a false self that is fueled by negative emotional reactions which, in turn, are maintained by habitual, incorrect thinking.

The false self is the master of illusions. To keep itself feeling alive, the false self has to work feverishly to keep us away from inner illumination. More simply, an understanding or heightened awareness from within undermines the false self's outward perception.

It is not what happens to us that causes us to be unhappy. Rather it is how we react to events that so clouds our judgments and perceptions that we will believe that what is happening around us is the source of our unhappiness. When we buy this lie, the false self wins. Nothing causes more discontentment than being unhappy about being unhappy.

True self, on the other hand, beckons us to collaborate with reality. True self wants to free us from painful, punishing emotions like guilt, fear, anxiety, resentment, anger, and others. Every second, true self is trying to get us to become aware that we are creating our own hell because we persist in our stubborn refusal to see heaven all around us.

Take one of our most pervasive modern day dragons—stress. Few would disagree that a stressful life is one that is in dire need of more happiness. A closer observation, however, will reveal that when we are stressed out, we are trying to force life to do what we want, when we want it done.

But isn't getting what one wants the way to be happy? Not necessarily. Getting what we want, or the anticipation of receiving it, may give temporary pleasure. But pleasure and happiness are not necessarily synonymous. More often than not, a preoccupation with pleasure-seeking is a good indication that an individual is estranged from an infinitely more enjoyable sense of well-being called happiness. "Happy people," I once read, "are not those who get everything they want; happy people are those who want what they've got." Besides, getting things—admiration, a degree, power, or a romantic relationship—are not in and of themselves a guarantee for happiness. Our true nature knows this.

> *"When you want what life wants, your wish is for life itself."*
>
> —GUY FINLEY
> THE SECRET OF
> LETTING GO

Contrary to the conventional wisdom of our modern society, happiness is not about getting or doing; happiness is about being.

Once we begin to shed all of our preconceived notions of what life has to give us in order to become happy; once we learn to see opportunity and growth in all of life's lessons; once we abandon our futile insistence that people and events must conform to our way of thinking; and once we accept reality as it presents itself to us, then and only then, will we begin to understand that feelings of happiness are always potentially present within us.

Understanding is key. Self-awareness, a prescription offered down through the ages by the greatest sages, is the only route to true happiness. Overcoming all the emotional and psychological pain created by the false self is an ongoing learning process. Expectedly, it is a process that will be violently resisted by our lower nature or false self.

Guy Finley further elucidates this point when he states: "If you will place learning before your pleasure, one day learning will come before your pain" (or your unhappiness).

So should you give up on your plans (i.e., desires) for the future? Are you to abandon your hopes for success? The answer is an unequivocal *no!* The only thing necessary to give up is the thought that one has to acquire something in order to be happy.

I believe our true self is the presence of God within each of us. Our true self knows what will make us truly happy. Our true self knows that if we will be still and quiet inside our own heads long enough, what we will begin to understand—with radiant clarity—is that we are already everything that we *need* to be.

With this awareness, we can begin to live our lives with the liberated notion that happiness has nothing to do with controlling people, circumstances, or the events of our lives. Happiness always comes only from within, and it is the only emotional state that our true self ever experiences.

Questions

1. In your mind, what does Guy Finley mean by the statement: "When you want what life wants, your wish is for life itself"?

2. When are you happiest? When you are experiencing the state of mind called happiness, have you later noticed that, for the most part, happiness seems to come and go independent of our desires to control when it arrives and when it exits?

3. If the surest route to unhappiness is focusing on what is wrong about your life, why do you suppose that so many people choose to focus on what is wrong with their lives?

4. Have you ever noticed how you feel when you are genuinely motivated to bring joy into the life of someone else?

5. How do you suppose you would feel if you spent most of your waking hours pursuing purpose rather than happiness?

ANGER
It Hurts You

A SEVENTY-SIX-YEAR-OLD GRANDMOTHER IS FRUSTRATED that her myriad acts of generosity toward her offspring are cavalierly taken for granted. . . .

An overworked, dedicated father has built up a simmering hostility toward his wife and children who spend his hard-earned dollars as soon as he earns them. . . .

A young, newlywed seethes with resentment that, immediately after the honeymoon, her new husband began making demands on her that were never mentioned during their yearlong courtship. . . .

The common thread that connects each of the above scenarios is the presence of a potentially dangerous emotion called anger.

None of us are impervious to the emotional and psychological impacts of the unsettling feelings associated with anger. It has extracted incredible costs from all of us. Expressed in outbursts, it has resulted in the lifelong estrangement of close family members and former cherished friends. When anger is pent up, we can seethe ourselves to ulcers, high blood pressure, and even heart attacks.

> *"He who the gods will destroy, at first they make angry."*
>
> —ANONYMOUS

Yet some mental health experts have maintained that protracted anger directed at other people and situations is actually anger directed at ourselves. When we allow ourselves to become engrossed in our anger or stubbornly cling to it, we are in fact punishing ourselves.

There is so much anger in our society: strangers shooting at each other or causing serious accidents on the nation's highways; hungry customers miffed that fast-food restaurants are not serving them quickly enough; and, even with a robust economy, it seems that almost everyone is angry that their dollars will not stretch far enough.

Why are we so angry? How do we get this volatile emotion under control so we can enjoy better emotional and physical health?

I believe one of the reasons that many of us are chronically angry is that we are suffering from the disease of entitlement. From our preschool, storybook days, we were constantly reminded that people "lived happily ever after." What a big lie that was! It was all childhood fantasy, but our subconscious minds seriously received the message over and over again that it *is possible* to live happily ever after. The indisputable truth reveals an opposite conclusion: no one lives happily ever after in this life. *Life is never without problems!*

Remember, it is what we believe deeply that governs our expectations of what life should give us. Most of us feel that life should not be filled with hassles, broken promises, premature death, financial strains, abused children, or dishonest people. Reality paints a different picture.

When we find that some person or event has left us feeling like a veritable cauldron of discontent, we can begin to take control of that triggering event by simply asking ourselves: where is the truth in the situation? If we are truthful with ourselves, we will readily admit that in every instance, it is our reaction—not the "offending" person or "irritating" event—that keeps us writhing in anger. But what is even more fundamental is that we fail to accept responsibility for our role in the hostility-provoking situation.

In the opening examples, truth would lead each party to one of the following conclusions:

- the incensed grandmother could set limits on her unappreciated generosity;
- the overworked father could discipline his spendthrift family members with a budget; and
- the young newlywed could be more assertive and could maturely discuss marital expectations with her husband.

When we seek the truth in any situation, the real source of our negative feelings emerges. Under the calming influence of an objective reality, we come to see ourselves as the originators and perpetuators of all of our negative emotions. The great thinker Anacharsis said it best: "Who is man's chief enemy? Each man is his own."

My friend, you have got some serious living to do. You will need to muster all possible energy and direct it toward the endless array of challenges that await you. Allowing some of your best energy to be sacrificed on the altar of vengeful anger is to make yourself your own mortal enemy.

You deserve better, infinitely better. When provoked by feelings of anger or its derivatives—frustration, resentment, or a need for revenge—move in the opposite direction with all deliberate speed to the refreshing tabernacle of truth. Reach in and take the cup of understanding. Drink from it and begin living with the wonderful knowledge that you need never be burnt again in the tormenting fires of relentless, raging anger.

Questions

1. Why do "the gods make angry him whom they will destroy"?
2. Have you ever noticed how physically and emotionally uncomfortable intense anger makes you feel? If it's the other guy who has you so riled up, why are you in so much pain?
3. How are fear and anger related?
4. Is anger possible without at least an undercurrent of fear?
5. Why is forgiveness a better option than a desire for revenge?

DIS + ILLUSION = REALITY
(Accept It!)

MARY T. FELL MADLY IN LOVE WITH JOSEPH W. THROUGH NINE intensely romantic months, she was led to believe that Joseph was prepared to commit to her for life. She returned early from an out-of-town visit with relatives and found Joseph in a compromising position with another woman in an apartment that she had jointly rented with him.

George S. loaned his best friend one thousand dollars to cover an emergency. A year later, the loan had not been repaid and the "trusted" friend had moved to another city.

In the above scenarios, individuals, because of unexpected circumstances, became disillusioned. Each had been traumatized by a conflicting picture of reality that left them feeling vulnerable. Each had to come face-to-face with aspects of daily living that contradicted their expectations.

If we live long enough, each of us will also experience disillusionment. That which we hoped for sometimes gets overshadowed by that which we seem to get.

For many, disillusionment is powerful enough a disincentive to extinguish the fires of their enthusiasm, to discourage their efforts, and to leave them feeling weak and small in the face of seemingly insurmountable odds.

As children, our optimism and boundless idealism allowed us to fantasize or daydream about a life of enchantment and fun. As we mature, reality will test our resolve with difficult or harmful situations. Bewildered, many will lower their expectations of life in an attempt to shield themselves from further disappointment and pain. But capitulating in the face of adversity is a serious mistake.

Dr. Gary Emery and James Campbell, coauthors of *Rapid Relief from Emotional Distress,* offer a powerful antidote for disillusionment's potential threat to our sense of well-being. Dr. Emery advises each of us to use what he has termed the *A.C.T. Formula.* The *"A"* stands for *accept.* When we are confronted with bad news or circumstances for which we were not prepared, our first line of defense should be to say "I accept it" over and over to ourselves. Acceptance is not tantamount to saying "I like it," "I approve of it," or "I will leave it uncontested." Acceptance is merely acknowledging that, at any given point in time, reality is presenting what reality is presenting. Frankly, reality does not conform to our wishes much of the time.

By accepting as real what is happening to us, we collaborate with reality. We embrace it for the lesson it is attempting to teach. We recognize that there will always be circumstances over which we have little control. But we don't stop there.

Next, the *"C"* represents our *choice* in how we will respond to an undesired state of affairs. We cannot control all of life's unfortunate incidents but we most definitely can control how we respond to them. Therefore, rather than becoming disillusioned or overwhelmed and ready to give up in the face of despair, we can switch gears and choose new visions from a unlimited list of possibilities that are available to us.

> *"Either you deal with what is the reality or you can be sure that the reality is going to deal with you."*
>
> —ALEX HALEY

Lastly, the *"T"* challenges us to *take action.* By taking action, we rob potentially debilitating occurrences of their devastating impact on our lives and harness our inner resources to move ahead in spite of our temporary setbacks.

Let us break the word *disillusion* into its two main components: *dis* means to do the opposite and *illusion* means to mock—a misleading image presented to the vision, or something that deceives or misleads intellectually.

So what the word means simply is this: when we are disillusioned, we are forced to face the truth that people and situations do not always conform to our wishes (i.e., our illusions). If we persist in believing that things should always go as we desire, we will continue to be mocked by the overshadowing reality that they do not.

These definitions explain the title of this essay: "Dis + Illusion = Reality." Reality is truth. Reality is what is real. We move ahead when we recognize the truth, accept the truth, and live by the truth. Any other approach to life will leave us baffled, bullied, and burdened.

The next time reality forces you to abandon your illusion of what ought to be, don't curse your fate or withdraw in defeat. Au contraire, choose to alter your picture of what is really real, graciously accept the lesson of the grand teacher (reality) and get busy drafting new, more realistic blueprints that will not find you wallowing in fantasy, but rather wondering in a world that really is *fantastic*!

Questions

1. Why do we judge other people by their actions and judge ourselves by our intentions?

2. How often do you confuse what you would like to receive from others (i.e., courtesy, thoughtfulness, understanding, forgiveness, etc.) with what we think we are entitled to receive?

3. The *A.C.T. Formula* is a wonderful tool to help us deal with disappointment. Can you think of a major disappointment from the past or present where you might employ this method?

4. When is fantasy our friend and when does it become our enemy?

5. Which of life's lessons are you still struggling to master (i.e., managing your finances, training others to treat you with respect, taking better care of your health, saying no when you really do not want to say yes)?

Dealing with Disappointment

LET'S FACE IT: NO ONE GETS THROUGH THIS LIFE WITHOUT PAIN. Life is tough. It extracts everything from us that it can. All of us at one time or another have thought, "Why is life so difficult, so wrought with disappointments, setbacks, unfulfilled dreams, aggravations, frustrations, etc.?"

I wish I had an easy answer to give. The Bible is replete with examples of human suffering. In *Will to Meaning* by Nazi concentration camp survivor Dr. Viktor Frankl, and in *The Plague*, by existentialist philosopher Albert Camus, we learn that human beings must find meaning in their suffering. All told, each of us must resign ourselves to the inescapable reality that suffering is part and parcel of the human condition.

> "*The common denominator in all emotional pain is a need to change current reality— which is unchangeable at the moment.*"
>
> —Dr. Gary Emery & James Campbell

The good news is that we create most of our suffering, especially the emotional pain experienced when we are suffering anxiety, fear, resentment, anger, and disappointment. I would like to offer a few suggestions that might help you to alleviate the lion's share of the pain that comes when you experience disappointment.

As was stated in the last essay, Emery and Campbell offer us their incredible formula for soothing the emotional pain caused by disappointment. The next time you are expecting someone or something to come through for you and you are left holding the proverbial bag, remember to use the *A.C.T. Formula*.

"*A*" stands for *acceptance*. Refuse to fight with reality; collaborate with it. For the moment, reality is doing what it is doing. By saying over and over to yourself that you accept the undesired situation does not lock you in or frustrate you. On the contrary, accepting— a simple exercise of your freedom to choose—opens channels inside your mind for other possibilities.

"*C*" stands for *choosing* your vision of what you would like to create as an alternative to your initial expectations.

For example, if you are rejected for a bank loan that would have capitalized your fledgling business venture, you may want to call others who were able to overcome this hurdle and are succeeding despite this commonplace practice.

"*T*" stands for *take action*. Nothing hurts more emotionally than a feeling of being trapped. Realize that you are never trapped, unless you choose to ally yourself with the forces that are working steadfastly to block your progress.

During this phase of utilizing the *A.C.T. Formula*, determined individuals also use the old "as if" model of thinking.

To use the above example, rather than succumbing to and wallowing in disappointment's emotional pain, serious entrepreneurs will repeat to themselves: "I will act 'as if' *I am* receiving the twenty thousand dollars that I applied for."

When one continues to invoke the "as if" principle, that individual activates the creativity of the right brain and stimulates the analytical powers of the left brain. With both hemispheres of the brain energized, options galore begin to surface.

When our re-energized entrepreneur becomes aware of the various alternative ideas for funding and writes them down—and withholds judgment of the merit of each—he or she now is prepared to apply a separate feasibility test to each idea.

Yes, life will always present us with disappointments. We do not control other people. And circumstances often engulf us when we are least prepared emotionally to handle them. Recognizing that we only control our reactions to people and circumstances, the sooner we accept the unexpected, the better.

Remember, however, that acceptance is only the first step. The remaining two—choosing a brighter vision and taking action steps to bring that vision to fruition—will leave us feeling more empowered, more positive, and definitely more like we are back in the game!

Questions

1. Someone has suggested that one of the most powerful reasons why people choose the easier route by habitually holding on to negative thoughts and emotions is because optimism sets one up for disappointment. What do you think about this statement?

2. When our sacred trusts are violated by someone dear to us, it rips our hearts apart. Why then is it unhealthy to keep reminding ourselves of the heartbreaking experience?

3. How does it feel to be disappointed with yourself? What strategy do you usually use to feel right again after you have performed beneath your own standards?

4. What valuable lessons from this essay could be taught to children?

· 5. When someone from the past has disappointed you, how might that past occurrence subconsciously limit your relationship with that person?

SHOULD, OUGHT TO,
AND *HAVE TO*
The Sources of Much of
Our Pain

A YOUNG MAN IN HIS EARLY THIRTIES STILL BEMOANS THE fact that his father abandoned him and his mother when he was three years old. At age thirty-two, he is unemployed, a high school drop-out, a drug abuser, and the father of two children, neither of whom he financially supports. When asked why his life is in shambles, he blames it all on his absent father: "He *should* have been there for me. My father ruined my life." Focus on the word *should*.

A frustrated young woman in her late twenties has been passed up for a position in a company where she has worked for five years. By her account, a less-qualified male was promoted over her. In fact, she had trained that male coworker. How does this young lady explain her predicament to herself? She states emphatically: "Those who run the company *ought not* to allow gender determine who gets promoted." Focus on the word *ought*.

A man in his forties is feeling pressured because all of his siblings have gone back to school to get advanced degrees, while he has gotten comfortable with his bachelor of arts degree in education. It is not that he has lost his passion for the classroom. Rather, it is that much of the conversation and praise are directed toward his more ambitious siblings at all the family gatherings. His wife and mother drop subtle hints that he is not living up to his potential. He has noticed lately that he is telling himself that he *has to* go back to school. Focus on the words *has to*.

Much of the emotional pain that we live with daily is born of our thoughts about what *should* have been, what *ought to* be, and what we *have to* do. The problem with this type of misguided thinking is that it forces us to live in a hell of expectations. We are choosing to hold out for a reality that does not exist, while rejecting a reality that does.

In the first scenario, the young man is deceptively convincing himself that a past created by a father's neglect is necessarily and unilaterally shaping his future. By his own faulty reasoning, he has given the ghost of an undesired circumstance from yesterday the power to haunt and limit his tomorrow. Only when the young man takes responsibility for his actions in the present and for shaping a course for the future will the irresponsible acts of his father begin to fade as a clouded memory.

In the second case, the young woman could also persist in a time-wasting rehashing of whether sexism should exist in the ideal workplace or she could direct her energies in more positive ways, by choosing from a variety of options available to her: 1) file a grievance within the company; 2) go to court; 3) seek a transfer within the company; 4) leave the company for one with bona fide non-discriminatory policies; 5) go back to school to acquire more skills; or 6) go into business for herself.

Her nonjudgmental acceptance of the reality that injustice has always found its way into the affairs of human beings could lower her blood pressure and raise her expectations of ultimately achieving her objective—being recognized and justly rewarded for her efforts. Accepting the fact of injustice is not the same as allowing it to go unchallenged.

Finally, for the middle-aged teacher caught in the insidious web of what he has to do in order to feel a sense of accomplishment, he has only to "seek the truth," for it alone will set him free. He could avoid the pitfalls created by foolish human pride. What his siblings accomplish or do not accomplish has absolutely nothing to do with how successful or fulfilled his life is. If climbing ambition's peakless ladder brings an individual fulfillment, climb on. But if finding fulfillment at one's present level of operating is rewarding, why indulge in a self-flagellating assault because of others' opinions?

In reality, we do not *have to* do anything but die. Everything else is a choice. Emotionally healthy people take responsibility for their choices. They avoid placing blame for their discontentment on other people or things outside of themselves.

Accepting life as we find it is always the beginning. Where we can improve our situation, we are free to do so. But knowing when to fight, when to flee, and when to flow seems to be the wisdom gained by those who have come to know that only by first *accepting reality* as we find it can we begin to *live life as we want it*.

Questions

1. Oftentimes, what we believe should happen for us does not. How might you alter your beliefs about what should happen to make yourself more content?

2. Life is not fair. Or maybe it is. We all ultimately get what we get. Does it help to tell yourself in advance that bad or tragic things will probably happen to all of us before we leave this life?

3. How might the quality of your life be improved from now on if you really decided that you would no longer compare your accomplishments with anyone else's?

4. Releasing our parents from our childish beliefs that they should have been perfect liberates us as well. What do you think?

5. In the best of all possible worlds, people are trustworthy, kind, noble, unselfish, and fair. Why is it so difficult to accept that we do not live in the best of all possible worlds?

 DISCOVERING THE SOURCE OF YOUR RESENTMENT TOWARD OTHERS

ALL HUMAN BEINGS ACT OUT OF THEIR EMOTIONS. ONE hundred percent of our behavior springs forth from some emotion. We are also social beings. So quite often, we make choices based on an analysis of how our actions will affect others. Much of our emotional imbalance (feeling upset) is born of attempts to win the approval of others. We spend countless hours of our precious time reacting to the agendas of our significant others.

The problem with being too other-directed is that it often leaves us feeling drained and unappreciated.

French writer Voltaire popularized the expression "best of all possible worlds." Indeed, if we lived in the best of all possible worlds, we would find that constantly stretching for others would leave us untorn because they would be stretching to meet us.

Unfortunately, it appears that selfishness has reached epidemic proportions in our "me-centered" society. Therefore, those who are burdened with the belief that other people's comforts should be of paramount importance are often left holding the proverbial bag.

I sincerely believe that it is more blessed to give than to receive. But I ask in earnest, what happens when an individual is constantly held hostage by a band of thieving takers? Where should we draw the line between the exhortation to be our brother's keeper on the one hand, and upholders of the first law of nature (commonsensical self-preservation) on the other?

Most of our stretching to create comfort for others springs from the strongest of all emotions—love. I believe that the happiest people among us are those who are centered in and primarily motivated by this cementing and uplifting emotion. But where is the line of demarcation that separates the realm of charitable concern for others from the emotionally healthy, self-protecting, self-loving concern for one's own best interest?

Much of what upsets us is rooted in our feelings of being taken advantage of by others. A lot of our anger and resentment reflects a perceived unbalanced equation. We feel out of kilter when we find ourselves giving and giving and giving. We become unsettled when others seem to always place their concerns and wants first (even when it is obvious that they do so at our expense).

So why do we make doormats of ourselves for others and complain about being walked on? How do we intelligently move in such a way that we communicate boundaries or limitations that others must honor? How do we control our own emotional need to depend so heavily on others that any deviation from their expectations of us provokes the frightening prospect that we might lose their love? How can we simultaneously secure for ourselves both the love and respect of our significant others?

It appears to me that the answer to all of the above questions is this: become your own "Rock of Gibraltar." Emotionally stand on your own two feet. Set limits on what you will allow others to take from you. But of equal importance, make sure you are not, in more subtle ways, bargaining for the emotional reinforcement that you are quite capable of giving yourself.

In many instances, our perceived charity is a facade. Many adults—attempting to escape the awesome burden of developing inner strength—unconsciously choose to enter unhealthy, parasitic relations to cipher the strength of others. Our resentments may well be the cover-ups that allow us to shine the light of blame on the bandit behavior of others while systematically ignoring their own emotional heists.

It is okay to set limits on others. It is okay to communicate your true feelings to others. It is absolutely okay to refuse to be used by others. But before you set sail on an unchartered sea of independence, make sure you have assumed the helm of the ship of your emotional needs, and that they are not still snarled in a tangled web of hidden, infantile dependency.

Say yes to the requests of others only when you are sure that yes reflects your genuine desire. To continue slavishly to honor the requests of others—without conscious awareness of why you are doing what you are doing—only perpetrates a vicious dependency cycle.

There is a healthier course. Become more aware of your private motives. Search deep within to discover whether you have taken responsibility for your own unmet needs. Decide today that others cannot construct your emotional bridge to a sense of well-being. Only you can do that. But when you are operating from an emotionally-sound foundation, you are then prepared not only to administer to self but your overflowing cup will allow you to give—without hostility and resentment—to others.

Questions

1. Where should we draw the line between the exhortation to be our brother's keeper and the upholders of the first law of nature (commonsensical self-preservation)?

2. What do you resent most about the behavior of your loved ones and why do you suppose that you have passively allowed yourself to be put upon?

3. Does it seem that the "me first" mentality is dominating human relations in our culture? How can you help to counter this obviously toxic societal trend without becoming a victim or feeling resentful toward others?

4. Have you done a self-analysis lately to discover which of your behaviors might be provoking resentment in others?

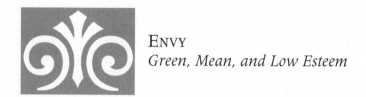

E<small>NVY</small>
Green, Mean, and Low Esteem

YOU PROBABLY MAY HAVE HEARD OF THE MAN WHO TOOK HIS wife to the doctor for a fourth time trying to discover the source of her allergic reactions to mink fur. After having run a battery of tests—all of which produced negative results—the exasperated physician asked the persistent husband, "Sir, why do you insist that your wife is allergic to mink fur?" "Doctor," the husband stated emphatically, "I know my wife is allergic to mink fur because every time one of the ladies in our neighborhood comes to show my wife a new mink coat, she gets sick."

The above story is a humorous depiction of how devastating an impact envy can have. It is simply born of a misguided belief in another's perceived advantage and the envious person's desire to attain the same position.

Envy is an ugly emotion. It is petty. It is mean-spirited. But most of all, it is a total waste of human energy. Envy wins nothing for the green-hearted. It is the preoccupation of the small-minded, the fearful, the faithless, and the unfortunate.

Many of us live and die by the "eleventh commandment" which states: "Thou shall not do better than me." We squander our precious time being overly concerned about what somebody else has or has accomplished, as if their situation has some causal relationship to our own predicament. We act as if another's success has an inverted effect on our chances of succeeding. We even calibrate our strategies for achievement based on the norm set by someone else. This is polar thinking at its worst!

An envious attitude creates in us a steady descent into a hell of negative emotions. The malice directed towards the object of our envy, in true boomerang fashion, invariably ends up leaving us feeling really horrible about who and what we've allowed ourselves to become. In the game of envy, there are no winners.

What has surprised me most about feelings of envy is that we rarely think of ourselves as being envious of others. We'll talk cavalierly and, at times, with pompous self-righteousness about the envious ways of others. Seldom do we see the green serpent in ourselves. Yet, we are all guilty of it at one time or another. Accepting this fact is the most important step to take in the direction away from envy's slimy swamp.

The next step is to try to identify the unconscious motivation for one's envy. It appears that at the core, envy is born of the mistaken belief that one cannot accomplish or attain on par with the envied party.

Envy is also an unconscious put-down of oneself. It is based on an erroneous assumption of limitations. It often has us focusing our attention in the wrong direction. And we become myopic because we are so emotionally involved with another's good fortune that we forget to stand back and get a better perspective or a broader view of the big picture of our own possibilities.

If we would turn our focus onto the unlimited potential and unique gifts that the Almighty has given to each of us, we would soon conclude that our lack of effort—not someone else's advantageous position—is the real source of our discontent.

Once we do the necessary introspection, take an honest inventory of our unactualized potential, and decide what it is that we really want and that we are willing to pay the price for it, we will soon discover that others' successes are not to be seen as sources of resentment; rather, they become sources of inspiration for the not-so-envious to pursue with a sense of purpose that which their hearts truly desire.

Questions

1. Of whom are you most envious? What additional knowledge about this person would cause your envy to be converted into compassion? How would the revelation that they have a terminal illness affect your envious attitude toward them?

2. Why do human beings have such a propensity for comparing ourselves to others? How can we rid ourselves of this bad habit?

3. How does it make you feel when you discover that someone you love very much is envious of you?

4. When you are "in your zone" and everything is going your way, how likely are you to resent someone else's good fortune?

GUILT
The Unnecessary Trip

GUILT IS AN UNNECESSARY TRIP THAT ALL OF US TAKE FROM time to time. Guilt makes us feel bad about ourselves but good about who we tell ourselves we are.

"Guilt," says John Roger and Peter McWilliams in their illuminating book, *Life 101,* "is anger turned inward." Why do we get so angry at ourselves for violating our personal moral codes? Because, as their book says, we want "to be right" at any cost.

The problem with guilt is that it solves nothing. Like its parent, anger, guilt is a by-product of the false self. It is a punishing emotion that does not have correction as its goal.

The progeny, guilt, is also born of a dreaded fear of the consequences of our actions or inactions. Oftentimes, it is the demon of unconscious unworthiness: unworthiness to be happy, unworthiness to achieve, unworthiness to be okay.

The ideal images of ourselves that we carry create only lip service to the ancient wisdom of the statement, "To err is human, to forgive is divine." We pervert the genius of this axiom by attaching our beliefs to a different conclusion: "I can't forgive myself for erring because I must hold onto the unrealistic notion that I can be perfect like the Divine."

I am no moralist, no preacher of the Gospels. I am not even an ethicist. But years of studying and observing human behavior has led me to the ineluctable conclusion that falling short of perfection is something that we do throughout our entire lives.

Does that mean that we should not have moral standards or that the Ten Commandments or other codes of conduct are not valuable guideposts that should be followed? The answer, obviously, is no.

Each of us finds contentment—to a greater or lesser degree— because we are striving to adhere to high standards of conduct. Ideals are worthwhile lighthouses that guide us through the darkness of life's myriad uncertainties.

All that I am attempting to convey in this essay on guilt is this: if you are human, you will make mistakes; you will transgress; and you will (hopefully, not too often) cause harm to others.

If you are human, you will sometimes not give your best effort. You will eat a second piece of cake while dieting. You will not be a perfect parent. You will say things to and about other people that are not kind. You will indulge yourself in behaviors that do not strengthen character. You will be tempted and, on occasion, you will yield to that temptation. As long as you dwell in the flesh, you will fall short of the glory.

But going on a guilt trip does not lead to the islands of salvation, liberation, or peace of mind. Getting angry at yourself for being human is like a dog being upset with himself for barking. Dogs bark. Human beings make mistakes. Human beings are human.

Lastly, the paradox of guilt's cyclical trip is that after the guilt has subsided and you have given yourself over to emotional self-flagellation, you have set the stage for more acts of self-indulgence (to do more of what you just punished yourself for). Purged, you are now ready to dive back into the pool of your excesses.

There is a better trip than the guilt trip. It is based on asking ourselves before we do the guilt-provoking deed(s), how am I going to feel about myself after I do it? What will be the likely consequences of my errant behavior? Why would I do something that would violate my own deeply held beliefs? Maybe it would be worthwhile to question whether or not we really believe what we say we believe.

While we are working on new strategies for mitigating the painful and wasteful side effects associated with feeling guilty, maybe we can take a second look at the only real cure for it—forgiveness. When you have violated your moral code, rattled your conscience, and unleashed anger's wrath against yourself, go sincerely but swiftly to the altar of forgiveness. With contrite heart and a new resolve to fix that which was broken, seek and administer to yourself the balm of forgiveness so that your spirit is free to do what is good because it leaves you feeling good and guilt-free.

Questions

1. It seems that no matter what we do, we are incapable of escaping our relentless tormenter, guilt. What are the greatest sources of guilt in your life?

2. One of the most obvious problems with guilt is that it keeps us living in the past. Why is it so important to live only in the present moment?

3. How might you expose the misguided and twisted logic that is the source of most of your guilty feelings?

PART III

"Rocks don't move in a swirling river."

—KEN BLANCHARD
AND SHELDON BOWLES
GUNG HO

SOLID VALUES HOLD OUR LIVES TOGETHER

OUR WORLD IS EXPERIENCING CHANGE AT AN UNPRECEDENTED rate. Many of the institutions that held our lives together are either crumbling before our very eyes or, for survival's sake, are themselves struggling with redefinition and transformation. In addition, community life that once defined how we would treat each other appears to be coming loose by the threads. Integrity, that virtuous standard that once regularly guided social intercourse, has far too often taken a back seat to get-all-you-can-any-way-you-can ethics.

Even something as sacred as human life itself has been cheapened and devalued because of our society's pathetic worship of such shallow idols as wealth, status, ego, and popular appeal.

Some of our elderly—who created many of the physical comforts that we now take for granted—are locked away to rot, while our children are thrown to the wolves of unscrupulous television and computer programs or, worse, to the anarchy of the streets.

Confusion, doubt, and uncertainty—coupled with relentless, out-of-control stress levels—have wreaked havoc on our minds, bodies, and souls. We want to be optimistic and focused on tomorrow's promise, but today's news keeps assaulting our spirits.

So where does one go for consolation? Where does one find peace of mind and real joy in living? How does one become centered and refocused? How might we live so that the sweet sounds of the songbird reflect our hearts' contentment and our human need to feel one with the majesty of life?

I am sure that the great philosophical thinkers, the mystics, and the meditators have far deeper insights into these profound questions than I do; but as a teacher of motivation and positive focusing, I would like to suggest that the first place one should go to find meaning and joy in life is inside oneself in order to get a closer glimpse of one's values.

Values. Values are what we are made of. Our values are who we really are. They guide us. Unlike our goals, our values are not only about tomorrow, they are also about today. Values are our rocks. Better yet, they are our roots that keep us firmly planted when the vicissitudes of tumultuous change and man's inhumanity toward man leave us feeling shattered and distrustful. Solid values are what keep us trying when wretchedness all around us seeks to derail our efforts at purposeful living.

Golden values cause our inner lights to shine through the all-consuming darkness created by setbacks, set-ups, and upsets.

Real values force us to face the inertia inside ourselves and to reignite our engines for more productive work and a greater desire to serve others.

Tried-and-true values forbid us from joining the status quo when it sanctions cruelty to others and cavalier attempts to rob any person of his or her God-given dignity.

Rock-solid values hold us together when we begin to fear or succumb to despair. Since that which confronts us has created the illusion of a threatening unknown, at first we may find ourselves trembling rather than standing steadfast.

Finally, "Rock of Ages" values strengthen our faith that after all is said and done, God is still in His heaven and much is *right* with the world.

In *Rhymes for the Land*, Manly Grant has captured in rhyme the message of this essay on values. I hope you are inspired by the beauty of his poetry.

Hold or Roll

Rocks hold firm while water's might
Sends pebbles rolling left and right.
Call pebbles rock? Set firm their goal?
First flash flood, still pebbles roll.
Not name, nor goal divide the two.
It's how they act. It's what they do.
Size dictates to stone, but you're in control.
Are you rock or pebble? Will you hold or roll?

Questions

1. We hear so much about the erosion of traditional social values today. But, in truth, individuals determine in each moment which

values they will continue to hold dear. Which values hold your life together?

2. Can you think of a few traditional social values that should be ushered onto the heap of history's excess baggage?

3. Which values will be needed for those occupying this planet in the next century? What role might you play in the inculcation of these new values?

4. Which values are driving you into the future?

SERVICE
The Price for the Space
We Occupy

AS THE BODY OF MOTHER TERESA, SERVANT OF CALCUTTA, was laid in state in India, all the world had an opportunity to focus on an incredible life of service. Mother Teresa, a Noble Prize winner, epitomized the joy and energy that are the by-products of purposeful living. She learned early in her life that it is indeed more blessed to give.

Two sparkling examples of individuals who have also learned the value of giving can be found in Nashville, Tennessee. Two sisters Mary Elizabeth Craighead (age eighty-four) and Sandra Olivia Smithson (age seventy-four) have done more in their postretirement years to help inner-city children to believe in themselves and their innate abilities than most of us do in a lifetime. Both educators and former principals, the two have successfully augmented the effectiveness of the local public school system.

During six weeks in the summer months and intermittently throughout the school year, they and a small cadre of teachers catch many inner-city children who might otherwise have fallen through the cracks of the public education system. The name of their enrichment program is PREP (Project Reflect Educational Programs). And prepped the young people are—for school and in some ways for life.

Smithson, the founder of the program, was quoted in a local newspaper, explaining the conversion that many of the children undergo. "We've dragged kids screaming into PREP and when it's over, we have to push them out the door. I remember one little boy in particular who finally learned to read. He ran outside yelling at the top of his lungs, 'I can read, Ma! I can read!'"

One child who came to PREP had already been labeled a slow learner by the school where she was regularly enrolled. After one summer in PREP, the little girl returned to that school, and by the end of the academic year, had made the honor roll.

Several hundred other children are also now mastering the fundamentals of reading, writing, and arithmetic because Mary Craighead and Sandra Smithson have chosen the path of service rather than selfishness.

Albert Einstein once stated that the only reason for human existence was to be here for the sake of other people. In his inspiring book, *Even Eagles Need A Push*, David McNally supports Einstein's conclusion: "Life is at its very best when people are willingly and happily contributing to each other."

For those who would shun providing service because of some implied inferior status that it imposes, Dr. Victor Frankl, who survived the Nazi concentration camps in World War II, reassured: "One need not be a servant to be able to serve."

Living in our modern, stressful, fast-paced world leaves many of us believing that we barely have time to take care of our immediate responsibilities. Helping others, while a worthwhile goal, is usually placed lower on the totem pole of our daily priorities.

Many of us, who have worked tirelessly to escape the throes of poverty, find no pleasure in the thought of returning to help those less fortunate. Yet, we must constantly remind ourselves that we were able to escape and to advance because of somebody else's blood, sweat, and tears.

Someone wisely stated that service is the price we pay for the space that we occupy on this planet. Well said. But service is not a chore, it is a privilege. If you want to bask in the company of the most joyful people on earth, just take the time to seek out the remaining Mother Teresas and the very busy Mary Craigheads and Sandra Smithsons. When you find them in the trenches, lend them a helping hand so that you, too, can become a powerhouse of energy and a storehouse of joy.

Questions

1. The Japanese have a term for collaborative efforts. It is *Keirutsu* meaning "interlocking units." How might the message of

this essay on service help you to become a node in the network of some worthwhile cause?

2. Why do you suppose that helpful people appear to have so much joy in their lives? What universal principles are at work when one cheerfully decides to give of himself or herself to help others?

3. This book is designed to assist you onto the path of more fulfilled living. Do you suppose it is possible to live a fulfilled life and yet be only concerned with one's own well-being?

4. List some of the immediate benefits that you can expect from getting involved with the business of helping others.

CREATIVE VISUALIZATION
What You See (in Your Mind)
is What You Get

IT IS TRUE. THE MENTAL PICTURES THAT DOMINATE OUR MINDS later become the living realities that constitute our experiences. Yet, we get to choose the pictures! Whether you are reading this essay or are having it read to you, know that you are endowed with creative powers so vast that they are difficult to explain. But please allow me to try. . . .

In Genesis, we are taught that each one of us (male and female) *"are made in the image and likeness of God."* God, we believe, is a Creative Spirit.

In Matthew 17:20, the great teacher said: *"Nothing shall be impossible unto you."* We are told that as spirits, we have the power to control matter. Thanks to the Heisenberg uncertainty principle, this profound conclusion by Jesus of Nazareth has been supported by the scientific community. For now, even the most stridently cynical scientists must concur that the mere "observing" of subatomic particles (i.e., matter) will alter them.

What then is the connection between Genesis 1:27, Matthew 17:20, and the topic of this essay, "Creative Visualization"? I believe the connection is this: if we are like God (a seminal, creative, and creating force in the universe), we must have some of God's power in us. Why else would the great teacher exalt us with such an overwhelming pronouncement as *"Nothing shall be impossible unto you"*?

Every human being is endowed with potential greatness. The emphasis here is on the word potential (from the Latin word *potens* which means "power"). Most people, it appears, live their entire lives without realizing this potential. *This need not be your fate!* If you will master the workings of your imagination, all manner of things can become possible for you.

> *"Fortis imaginatio generat causum."*
>
> Translation:
>
> *A strong imagination begets the thing itself.*

It has been written that everything is created twice—first in our minds and then in reality. Earl Nightengale, the late expert on human potential, electrified his audiences by repeating the provocative statement: "I become what I think about all day long." It is axiomatic, with mathematical certainty, that each of us is that which we focus our thoughts on, and the mental pictures those thoughts create.

Dr. Joseph Murphy, a noted metaphysician, taught that human beings are equipped with an unlimited powerhouse called the subconscious mind. The subconscious mind, according to Dr. Murphy, is a genius-servant. It takes orders from your conscious mind, especially when they accompany strong emotions ("As a man thinketh in his heart, so is he") and clear pictures (i.e., creative visualization).

For example, if you harbor feelings of resentment, carry pent-up feelings of anger, or worry incessantly about money matters, not being loved or appreciated, or lagging behind others, your subconscious mind may receive these thoughts and their attendant negative images in such a way that the physical brain will begin, through an intricate system of communication signals, to produce toxic chemicals that adversely affect the body's immune functions, thereby making you susceptible to disease. Those negative thoughts created first in your mind soon produce real-life consequences. One great student of psychoneuroimmunology concluded: "Disease in our thoughts and emotions leads to disease in our bodies."

The subconscious mind is equally equipped to transform our mundane, unexciting, and pain-filled lives into ones that are focused, goal-directed, challenging, and far, far more enjoyable.

The subconscious mind produces what we believe at the deepest level of our being. We cannot fake it. What we sincerely believe about ourselves, our abilities, and the direction that our lives will take eventually will all be manifested. From the concept (mental picture) to the concrete (reality), we are either creating health, wealth, loving relations, high energy, joy, peace of mind, and enthusiasm or we are creating anger, resentment, illness, ingratitude, selfishness, boredom, low energy, and, possibly, premature death.

If you are wondering how to get started, may I suggest that you find a secluded spot (your favorite, most comfortable place); close your eyes; take ten deep breaths; totally relax your body; slow down your thoughts; and just experience, in your solitude, the bliss of being alive. Say to yourself several times: "nothing matters, no guilt or regrets about yesterday, no anxiety or worries about tomorrow." Just get into the golden moment. *Focus only on the present moment that you are experiencing right now*!

Allow your thoughts to create mental pictures. On the mind's screen, see what it is that you want to accomplish or experience. See the new home or the new car. See yourself getting along with family members or friends with whom you have recently quarreled. See yourself enjoying your work. See yourself going back to school or college (regardless of your age or circumstances). See yourself moving with high energy. See your bank statement reflecting a wealthier person. See yourself handling anger with calmness, strength, and straightforwardness. Now, add your own pictures.

If you are left-brain dominant, you may have difficulty with this approach to programming your mind. No sweat. If seeing is problematic for you, try hearing that which represents the realization of your dreams. Hear the sounds you make when something wonderful happens to you. Think about each thing that you want to accomplish and simply hear the sounds associated with achieving that which you hoped would come to pass.

If seeing and hearing do not get you in a positive programming state, then try to focus your thoughts and energy on producing the feelings associated with enjoying the experience of the universe which gives to you the desires of your heart.

Creative visualization is also an excellent way to interrupt negative, depressing, self-limiting, and counterproductive thoughts. Since you now know that your thoughts create mental pictures, which, in turn, can become reality, why not choose to construct pictures and outcomes that lift your spirit and get you focusing on what you do want rather than what you do not want.

It is all about choice. With each moment, we can choose to live lives filled with positive expectations by holding onto visions of what is possible or we can cling to pictures of unhappy situations, underachievement, and pain. The choice is ours.

Ultimately, creative visualization allows us countless opportunities to be cocreators of our own destinies. We really do get out of life what we see ourselves getting. Through creative visualization, we can ameliorate the negative, self-defeating filmmaking of the past and begin producing more positive movies for the future: movies where we consciously assign to ourselves the starring role in our lives and take responsibility for the consequences of our actions, both positive and negative. As the empowered directors of our own plays, we can issue lines through our persistent thoughts which will cause us to behave in new ways, ways that say to ourselves and to all the world: *I am created in the image and likeness of almighty god.*

From now on, I will use this awareness to create pictures for my life that inspire and motivate me to greater heights of achievement. Fear and failure will no longer control me. From this day forward, I will live with the confidence-boosting words found in Matthew 17:20: *"Nothing shall be impossible unto you."* Now, let the film roll!

Questions

1. Nancy Rosanoff, author of *Intuition Workout,* says: "Our imagination is similar to an electrical wire. An electrical impulse is sent through a wire, and the current flowing through the wire creates a negative field, which pulls more energy toward it. With our imagination we begin by directing images toward a goal. Our directed imagination has created a magnetic field which pulls in energy from another source." If you accept Rosanoff's statement as valid, what would you like to create in your life that will increase your spiritual health, wealth, and happiness?

2. Why is it important to see clearly where you would like to go, see it often, and want to get there with a burning desire?

3. How does daydreaming differ fundamentally from conscious, wide-eyed, purposeful creative visualizing?

4. What would you like to "see" disappear from your life? How might using the practice of imagining or creative visualization help

you to eradicate those aspects of your life that rob you of your sense of well-being?

5. Children often entertain themselves with games that contain the phrase "play like" (e.g., "Let's play like we're cowboys and Indians"). A more adult version of this game would be "act as if." If you thought you would not fail, what might you begin to create by completing the following sentence: I am going to act as if
_____.

OPTIMISM
How Winners View Life

WHY WRITE AN ESSAY ABOUT OPTIMISM? WHO NEEDS another discussion about the importance of maintaining a more positive mental attitude? What is left to be said? What if I am a person who is comfortable being negative or pessimistic most of the time? Isn't expressing dissatisfaction with life's unending parade of catastrophes and upsets just "telling it like it is?"

Aren't people with characteristically cheery dispositions a little bit out of touch with reality? How can a sane person read the daily newspapers or watch the evening news and allow his/her thoughts to continue undaunted with a stubborn optimism?

Few would disagree that although the evening news tends to focus disproportionate attention on man's inhumanity toward man, there are more than ample reasons to bemoan all the evils that men do.

So why choose to be optimistic about one's life, one's possibilities, or one's world? Why adopt what one writer calls "the secret belief of the inverted paranoid who believes that the entire universe is conspiring to do him/her some good?" Why would a practical person, endowed with sound reasoning abilities, persist with hopeful beliefs in an uncertain and often tragic world?

I believe that in spite of all the aridity and disenchantment, optimists have learned that they are living, for the most part, the life that they rehearse in their own minds.

The term *optimism*, according to the *Random House Thesaurus*, is "confidence." Optimism is seeing the good side of things. Optimism is encouragement. Optimism is having a happy expectancy (a belief that one's outcome will be positive). But most important of all, optimism is having trust in the future.

"Nobody, as long as he [she] moves about among the chaotic currents of life, is without trouble."

—CARL JUNG

This last definition is the bottom line. Someone once wrote: "The human being can live more than three weeks without food. Maybe three days without water. But not three minutes without hope. Hope is the fuel of optimism." Optimism is the foundation for extraordinary accomplishments.

Looking at those individuals—past and present—who have achieved enviable heights of greatness, one hears repeatedly the words of tough-minded optimists:

"The sister of misfortune, hope
In the under darkness dumb,
Speaks joyful courage to your heart.
The day desired will come."
—Alexander Pushkin, 1824

"Out of the sighs of one generation are kneaded
the hopes of the next."
—Joaquin Machado DeAssis, 1906

"I'm here, I exist and there's hope."
—Vernon Jarrett, 1965

"The first thing we are going to do in here, children, is an awful
lot of believing in ourselves."
—Marva Collins, 1990

"I see the cup as half-filled and I get busy
filling up the other half."
—General Colin Powell, 1996

"I was determined to do it . . ."
—Oprah Winfrey, 1996

"I wanted to grow up and win a championship
over the pros."
—Tiger Woods, 1997

"I believe we can win [another NBA title]
with what we have."
—Michael Jordan, 1997

It appears that those who have gotten and are getting what they want from life are the optimists, "the inverted paranoids who believe the universe is conspiring to do them some good." What are some of the techniques of these indomitable spirits? Alan Loy McGhinnis, author of *The Power of Optimism*, believes that the following are common tactics used by winners and optimists:

1. interrupt negative trains of thought;
2. keep focused on the desired outcome;
3. seek partial solutions;
4. accept failure as temporary;
5. laugh at themselves;
6. feel that they are bigger than circumstances;
7. radiate goodness to others;
8. stay determined;
9. "write their worries in the sand";
10. sincerely believe that where there is a will, there is always a way.

Yes, life is incredibly tough on us. So what? Winning against the odds is victory made sweeter. As the inhabitants of the twenty-first century on this earth, we do not have to create anew an optimistic view. All that is necessary is to look back and build up on the incredible optimism of those who went before us.

The optimistic call to greatness resides in each of us. It will be activated when we adopt the attitude of that great conquering leader Hannibal, an indefatigable optimist, who emphatically stated: "We will either find a way or make one." Because of his tough-minded optimism, Hannibal overcame incredible odds. So can you!

Questions

1. History is replete with the incredible accomplishments of optimists. Why do you suppose tough-minded optimists are able to defeat incredible odds and achieve spectacular results?

2. How has the optimistic view of life helped you recently?

3. Why do you suppose that many people equate pessimism and realism?

4. How might you go from thinking pessimistic, self-defeating thoughts to optimistic, the-sky-is-the-limit thinking?

LISTENING
The Only Way to Be Heard

WE ARE A SOCIETY OF TALKERS. EVEN FOR THOSE OF US WHO are not so loquacious, listening to others is a rare gift.

Generally, we are not listening with concentration to the words of others. Equally as alarming, we are not even listening to the quiet wisdom that comes from our own inner-voice.

Much of the reason for our diminishing ability to focus on what others are saying to us is that we live in a noise-saturated world. Daily, we are bombarded with messages from every medium conceivable: television, radio, billboards, bus advertisements, sales people, organizations, etc. The list is endless.

Our pace is faster, so we move into changing environments with increased rapidity. There are myriad faces in the crowd and everybody's got a story to tell. We hear so much. But hearing and listening are not synonymous terms. Listening is the process by which we distill and discern what we hear.

Listening takes hearing to a higher, more meaningful level. We listen to people and messages that we value. We listen to those that we would transform. We prick our ears for those in whom we have a vested interest. We unintentionally block out all other noise stimuli to focus our hearing attention on that which we think matters to us. The key is having the good judgment to know when to listen and when to block information from our sphere of concentration.

Those who are not proactive, who do not exercise the discipline to discern what is worth listening to and what constitutes information overload, end up poor listeners because the mind's capacity to focus simultaneously on many diverse, often conflicting messages becomes strained.

Becoming a good listener is a necessary predicate for success in our modern world. It has probably always been so, but today's achiever must face the added challenge of fine-tuning his or her capacity for sorting the treasures from the rubbish. Most of what is thrown at us today is pure rubbish!

In addition, good listening is the antidote for all misunderstandings. Renowned corporate trainer Dr. Stephen Covey advises: "Seek first to understand and then to be understood." We understand another's point of view when we choose to listen with an open mind and a caring heart. Among the many rewards we can expect after taking this approach is that the other party will be primed to listen to our side of the story.

Here are seven more good reasons to develop your listening skills:

1. Good listeners enhance the quality of their own lives by giving themselves a reprieve from their concerns and worries.
2. Good listening is therapy for both the listener and speaker.
3. Good listening promotes intimacy.
4. Good listening encourages patience.
5. Good listening furthers the aims of deeper understanding. Understanding is vertical and infinite; the more we listen, the more insights come to us.
6. Good listeners feel more powerful and exercise more control of themselves.
7. Good listeners triumph in an age of information. In the business world, they gain the competitive advantage because of the quality of information that they receive and later disseminate.

Few would argue that ours is a gregarious society and it often appears that those who are glib of tongue take home more symbols of achievement. But don't be fooled. Communication is a two-way street, and those who continue to be verbose, when listening would be more appropriate conduct, soon discover that others begin to see them as self-serving and shallow.

Everyone wants to be heard when it's their turn to speak—even the shy and the introverted. Many a profound statement has followed their prolonged silence. Only those willing to wait patiently and listen become the beneficiaries of their wisdom.

So do you really want to be heard, to be understood by others? Then decide today that you do not have to add inordinately to life's noise pollution. You can choose, instead, to become a member of that charmed minority that enjoys the secret knowledge that the best way to be heard, understood, valued, and appreciated by others is to "lend them your ears." If you will do so, they, in turn, will choose to praise your ideas, not bury them.

Questions

1. Ours is a society of polar thinkers. Everyone seems to be concerned with who's on top and who's on the bottom, who's in and who's out, and who's winning and who's losing. This narrow-mindedness has also corrupted our collective ability to listen to each other. Typically, how much of your conversation is focused on the statements of others?

2. How might empathetic listening affect the self-esteem of the individual who is attempting to communicate with you?

3. How does disciplined listening increase the probability that others will understand your point of view?

4. How does impatience, self-centeredness, and a desire to dominate others undermine effective communication?

5. If becoming a good listener suddenly became a priority for you, what would be your first step in developing this very valuable skill?

CONTROLLING YOUR
SUGGESTIVE ENVIRONMENT
(Because Birds of a Feather . . .)

WE'VE ALL HEARD THE OLD AXIOM "BIRDS OF A FEATHER flock together." But have you ever asked yourself why they do?

Being aware of who we are choosing to spend our quality time with and knowing these individuals wield powerful influence on our thoughts and actions is something worth pondering. Consciously or subconsciously, we are building lives for ourselves that we will come to believe are heavens or hells. A preview of the coming attractions that we call the future is being shaped in great measure by the people whom we allow to share our sacred space today.

Think about it. How did your spouse (or significant other) respond the last time you enthusiastically mentioned an idea that could lead you back to school, or to opening a business, or to controlling your weight, or whatever?

Get the picture? *Those who are close to us are in a powerful position to add wind to our sails or to snuff the life out of our enthusiasm.* How many times have you heard a sibling or a so-called friend undermine you with the popular sapper, "So you think you're all that now?" How often have you felt the sting of the discouraging remark, "You've got to be crazy to think you can do that?" Other dream-busters include: "you are too old"; "you are not known well enough"; "they wouldn't listen to that"; "it will never work"; and "why don't you get yourself a real job" (when you're exploring the world of entrepreneurship).

The people with whom we associate can make or break us. They can convince us that we don't have the right stuff to live life as we dream it should be lived or they can help create a synergy that convinces us that all manner of things are possible.

Many of our relatives and so-called friends have given up on their dreams. Now, they have climbed aboard our ships with the ignoble intentions of sinking them. Who we choose to listen to is always an indication of whether we secretly intend to sink or sail. If we are constantly hearing words of limitation and defeat from those with whom we choose to associate, our deepest intentions or unconscious unworthiness is being revealed to us. If, on the other hand, the words of our companions are as cheering throngs, we know that our own will to succeed is strong indeed.

It is of paramount importance that we choose positive, encouraging, supportive, dream-sharing friends and associates. Even among family members, it is important to separate those who provoke arguments, hostility, and insecurity from those who are mutually supportive.

How, you might be asking, does one deal with family members with whom one is forced to share space? The answer is simple; if they are negative, energy-draining, nothing-is-ever-right-or-good-enough individuals, you may not want to limit their place in your heart but, for survival's sake, you must limit their space in your head.

Controlling our suggestive environments is our responsibility and ours alone. Our lives are our kingdoms. Just as we would not invite wild, vicious predators into the places where we live, we would want to guard against those who come to drain the life out of our best intentions or efforts.

The flip side of the coin is equally valid; it is imperative that we do not allow our ill-tempered moods to cloud out the sunshine of others' enthusiasm for their ideas or dreams. If we cannot encourage their efforts, we can at least acknowledge their good intentions.

Human beings are social animals. Contrary to the tenets of rugged individualism or to the obsessive preoccupations of a narcissistic "Me Generation," we desperately need each other. All of nature reflects the inevitability of social networking. It is a part of the Divine Plan that we operate best when we recognize our interdependence. The late, great Dr. Martin Luther King Jr. said it best: "We are caught up in a web of mutuality." John Donne also captured the essence of our need for each other with his famous line: "No man is a island; no man stands alone."

So, since we must depend on each other, why not choose to be and to surround ourselves with positive energy? Doing so will cause us and our companions to soar with expectations for life's limitless possibilities and then we will come to understand why birds of a feather need to flock together.

Questions

1. Who are two or three persons in your life whose counsel you most value?

2. Next to the negative, critical advisor that dwells within your own head, who has discouraged you the most from pursuing your dreams? Does this person (or persons) continue to wield strong influence over your thinking? Why or why not?

3. Can you remember as a preteen or later as a teenager how much power peer influence had over you? Do your present peers inspire you or invite you to a life of mediocrity and low achievement?

4. While it may be both foolish and irresponsible to blame others for our failures, in doing so, we are at least recognizing the power of their influence. How does taking personal responsibility for all your choices limit the negative influence—past and present—of significant others?

GOALS
Getting On A Line for Success

WHAT DO JOHN H. JOHNSON, HERMAN J. RUSSELL, CLARENCE Smith, Edward Lewis, Nathan Conyers, and Earl G. Graves have in common? Answer: they are all devoted to the practice of goal setting.

Goal setting gives us direction. It helps us to get focused. It fuels the fires of enthusiasm. It beckons us to look deep within ourselves for the strength "to reach beyond our grasp," says *Ebony* magazine's Johnson.

Although goal setting is a guiding principle in all worthwhile motivational training, as a process, it must be well thought out. There are steps leading to goal setting and goal-attainment that must be meticulously followed.

Those who have developed the good habit of setting long-range and short-range goals know that the human brain has a cybernetic function and operates best when this function is engaged properly.

First, it is essential to know that conflicting internal motivations will cause a wasteful dissipation of energy needed to bring one's goals to fruition. Anticipating this potential for self-sabotage, successful goal-setters always know, first, what their highest priority is and, second, that each goal set must be in harmony with this transcending priority.

Next, it is of paramount importance to know why one hopes to attain a particular goal. Compelling reasons—which emanate from the core of one's value system—summon passion, that seemingly inexhaustible energy supply that makes ordinary people do extraordinary things.

Third, those who have mastered the art of goal setting have clear pictures of how accomplishing their goals will effect their lives. By creatively visualizing their goals as already accomplished, they not only begin their movement with the sweet assurance of guaranteed success, they also enjoy the intense feelings that such pictures elicit and the confidence to continue on a winning path.

Fourth, to borrow from the discipline of physics, remember Isaac Newton's first law of motion: "An object at rest tends to stay at rest. An object in motion tends to continue in motion at constant speed in a straight line." To get on a line to success and stay there, one must maintain his or her momentum during those prescribed times of activity.

Goal setting virtuosos are also realistic about their chances of successfully attaining their goals because they always take an inventory of themselves, their resources, and the possible obstacles that they may encounter. In addition, those adept at goal setting know that modest, incremental goals, that are routinely celebrated when achieved, lay the foundation for greater success in the future.

Dr. B. F. Skinner, a behavioral psychologist, advanced the notion that positively reinforcing behavior increases the probability that such behavior will reoccur and with greater frequency. Stated simply, whenever you accomplish a goal, large or small, always give yourself a reward.

Finally, remember the wisdom of British Prime Minister Winston Churchill, who advised his imperiled countrymen during World War II to "Never, never, never, never give up." Have contingencies; be flexible; retreat and rest when necessary, but never give up!

When we go after our goals with a burning passion, we activate the powers of our superconscious mind. We ally our energies with the causal force of the universe. We literally become unstoppable!

So after prayer and/or meditation, conjure up your goals. Write them down, and write a date of completion next to each one.

If you have done all of the above, the only thing left to do is to follow the wisdom of the late, great Lou Ora Smithson, who shared her modus operandi with an inquiring reporter: "I pray as if everything depends on God and then I work as if He didn't exist."

In our study of mathematics, we learned that the shortest distance between two points is a straight line. In the game of goal setting and goal-attainment, the straight line is effective goal setting. Follow this line and success will follow you everywhere you go.

Questions

1. Why do you suppose that writing one's goals down is so critical to achieving them?

2. Where do most people fall short on the continuum from goal conceptualization to goal-attainment? Why?

3. If you do not have three important goals and their dates of completion placed where you can see them two or three times a day,

please decide at this moment that you owe it to yourself to do so. Why is it important to stop everything and begin this process now?

4. Why is it necessary to reward your progress in increments (short steps) rather than waiting for the end result before celebrating the attainment of your goals?

 WALK THE TALK

FROM TIME TO TIME, I HAVE TO CHECK MYSELF OUT TO SEE IF I am doing what it takes to accomplish my goals. It is easy to tell ourselves what we intend to do. Many people take great pride in trying to impress others with the magnitude of their grand plans. Some will talk endlessly about what they are going to do, where they are going to be, and what they are going to have.

We all know individuals like this. Whenever we encounter them, they are getting ready to do something spectacular or, at least, better than the average.

After a while, being around such individuals becomes intolerably boring. After we've listened with keen interest over and over, we grow weary with undertakings that never get undertaken. We grow impatient with individuals who love to hear themselves talk. The truth about their real intentions eventually turns on a light of awareness inside of us; we then resolve that enough is enough.

Observing the fake, the false, and the fantasy in others is done with relative ease. We waited on several occasions for action steps to follow lip action. A pattern was established. We judged the person making the false promises to himself/herself to be insincere. Then we move on.

Seeing the faker in others is easy. But what about seeing the pretender in ourselves? What about our own hollow attempts to impress others with what we plan to do? How many times have we told ourselves that we are going to accomplish this task or that, knowing full well that the necessary effort would not be forthcoming? So, other than the vain attempt to impress others with what we are capable of achieving, why do we talk endlessly about what we are going to do?

I believe the answer is low self-esteem. We are trying to help ourselves feel good about who we are and what we are made of. The irony of talking the talk but not walking the talk becomes clear. Neglecting to follow through with plans that we have announced to others (or to ourselves) does not raise our esteem, it lowers it. We also respect ourselves less.

High self-esteem is more than just temporarily feeling good about ourselves. The good feelings that our talk generates are ephemeral or short-lived. Like a drug's effect wearing off, our moods plummet to lower and lower levels each time we attempt to do with words that which only disciplined action can accomplish.

> *"It's time for a checkup from the neck up."*
>
> —Zig Ziglar

Sustained high self-esteem has as one of its most essential components a thing called *integrity*, which means "wholeness" or "completeness." When our words and deeds are so integrated with purposeful action that we only say what we truly intend to do, we have integrity. Our integrity helps us to feel really good about who we are.

My grandmother used to recite the poem, "Cheating The Man in the Glass." I don't recall all the lyrics, but I distinctly remember the poem's potent closing stanza:

> You may fool the whole world down the highway of life
> And get pats on the back as you pass.
> But your final reward will be heartaches and tears
> If you've cheated the man in the glass.

The one person that we can never really fool—not even those most gifted in denial—is ourself.

Success in any venture—large or small—demands its payment in advance. There are no easy routes to take. We retain a degree of self-respect when we choose to seal our lips until we're ready to put forth the necessary energy to transform our talk into action. But when we do muster the resolve to get busy (busy walking the talk and not just talking it), we boost our chances of succeeding and, in the process, lift our self-esteem.

Questions

1. How has lying to yourself caused you grief in the past?

2. Why do so many people have such a propensity for wanting to build themselves up in the eyes of others? What is the motivation behind this counterproductive posturing?

3. One great mind once said: "There is no such thing as bragging. You are either telling the truth or you are lying." When, if ever, is bragging healthy behavior?

4. If you have fallen into the habit of talking about what you intend to accomplish more than working to accomplish what you talk about, answer this question: "Will you just do it or continue to doubt it?"

PERSISTENCE
The Pill That Pushes

I ONCE HEARD A SERMON ENTITLED "HOLD ON." THE PREACHER made a number of good points but the most compelling was his advice to those who were becoming discouraged in their quest for better health, more wealth, and more happiness.

At the climax of his moving message, that wise man of the cloth drove home his point with the hope-filled reassurance: "When you get to the end of your rope, tie a knot and hold on." He had honed in on the central theme of all persistence: hold on.

If you have ever set a goal, especially a lofty one, you have experienced those moments of utter doubt. Despondent, you probably began questioning yourself and your judgment for having set a seemingly unrealistic goal with an equally questionable timetable for completion. In frustration, you may have told yourself that whatever you initially thought, it was now clear that maybe it was not worth all the effort.

It does seem that when we go after something that our hearts really desire, persistent, invisible, and antagonistic forces mount their ingenious and protracted opposition to counter our every move. Frustration has caused many erstwhile efforts to be abandoned when a little more advancement would have rendered them victories. But intractable resistance to our efforts can wear down our spirits and leave us walking away from that which we dreamed of seeing come to fruition.

You might now be asking the question what must I do? The pain of perennial disappointment is a punishing pill to swallow. This is true especially when one feels exasperated after much honest effort. However, the prescription pill for pushing ahead is persistence. Persistence is the offspring of passionate desire. That is why one brilliant writer wrote: "In order to get what you want, you must first know what you want and then really want what you want." His point is clear; only strong desire and clear vision can guide us through the storms that always seem to rage when we set out on the journey of accomplishment.

Persistence forthrightly reminds us that no matter how much effort or time you have invested, it is not done until it is done. In regards to the question "how much more must I give to achieve my goal," the answer is unequivocal—as much as it takes to get the results that you are seeking.

Also, our level of persistence is correlated to our level of commitment to the goal(s) that we seek to accomplish. Commitment means taking a serious inventory of self and doing more than a cursory study of what realizing a particular goal would entail—up front.

Our willingness to be persistent is the only way to measure daily how important accomplishing a goal continues to be. Many of us stagger into clouded notions of what we half-heartedly think we want to achieve. Then, when we meet the inevitable resistance that tests our resolve, we cave in. This is not how winners approach their goals. Winners anticipate turbulence. When they are getting the airplane of their desires off the ground, they know that only the added fuel of persistence will blast them through the mounting turbulence. They increase velocity. They rise above when those with weaker intentions fall by the wayside.

Whatever you pursue, pursue it with persistence. Go with the attitude that there is no turning back. When discouraging thoughts beckon you to abandon your hopes and dreams, reach down deep into the well of your being to summon one of your spirit's bravest warriors. There, in your darkest hour, you will observe that the tide is turning in your favor. Then, you will come to believe that the greatest forces of opposition will ultimately be defeated when faced by an unconquerable persistence.

Questions

1. From where does the desire to persist with one's goals or objectives come?

2. What is the path of least resistance? How might taking this route undermine successful completion of your goals?

3. Can you remember a time in the recent past when holding on a little longer would have given you the outcome that you desired?

4. How might family and friends be recruited to help you to persevere until your goal has been attained?

5. What role does fear play in the decision to give up prematurely?

POSITIVE REINFORCEMENT
The Right Honey for the Bees

ONE OF THE MOST EFFECTIVE WAYS TO ALLOW YOURSELF TO enjoy more success in life is to master the art of positively reinforcing one's desired behavior. When properly applied, positive reinforcement is also one of the most effective techniques known to help modify the behavior of others.

Psychologist B. F. Skinner distinguished himself by his theories and experiments which advanced the notion that behavior is a function of its consequences. Stated in laymen's terms, to a great degree, each of us will repeat the behaviors with which we associate pleasure.

Conversely, we also avoid behaviors that are followed by painful or undesirable consequences. Tasks that make us feel uncomfortable or inconvenienced are systematically shunned. In a word, if an immediate outcome is not enjoyable, most human beings would just as soon not engage in the antecedent behavior.

What are the implications of this insight? They are nothing short of profound for those who wish to replace counter-productive habits with behaviors that lead to more health, wealth, and an overall sense of accomplishment.

As children, one of the ways that we learned was through operant conditioning—acting in ways that would elicit positive responses from our parents and others. As adults, we can consciously condition our behavior, rather than merely respond to the dictates of others.

"People do what they do because of what happens to them when they do it."

—AUBREY C. DANIELS, PH.D.

BRINGING OUT THE BEST IN PEOPLE

For example, if an individual decides to go into business for himself/herself, the first priority should be to map out a strategy from A to Z which would include (among other things): finding an unmet need, studying trends, researching the broader marketplace, identifying capital resources, writing a business plan, etc.

In order to assure success, the individual would reward himself/herself for each step along the path towards establishing the new venture. By setting modest, incremental goals and acknowledging the successful completion of each step with positive reinforcement, the entrepreneur increases the probability that he or she will continue to act in a manner that improves the likelihood that the enterprise will succeed.

If an individual desires to replace a particular bad habit (e.g., getting angry quickly, not exercising, eating junk food, or wasting money), then that person needs to identify the good habit that stands diametrically opposite of the undesired behavior. Then, he or she begins the process of rewarding any behavior which increases the likelihood that a more productive habit is being formed.

If desired behavior is reinforced long enough, a new habit will be formed. Psychoneurologists claim that a new neural groove will be created in the brain.

Positive reinforcement works equally well on our spouses, children, coworkers, bosses, and neighbors. Catch someone doing something that pleases you, then consciously choose to direct positive energy in the form of praise or appreciation and watch the magic of operant conditioning go to work. A wonderful example of this phenomenon is found in a very popular book on the market entitled *The Celestine Prophecy.* The author graphically illustrates the point by demonstrating that plants that receive concentrated attention from human beings grow larger and have more nutrients than those that are ignored. Where we focus the most attention (or energy), we amplify or cause an increase. Praising or directing positive attention toward someone is a sure-fire reinforcer.

Getting the best from ourselves and others is an ongoing challenge to say the least. But knowing that beating up on ourselves and degrading others are not the best approaches to changing behavior is cause for celebration.

No, we are not Skinner's rats in a maze. To claim that human behavior is ever predictable with mathematical certainty is pure exaggeration. But the knowledge that we can alter harmful or nonproductive behavior patterns in ourselves and positively influence the behavior of others with some predictability is indeed empowering.

Questions

1. Think of three of your most persistent, entrenched habits. What enjoyment can be associated with each?

2. How might the ideas of this essay on positive reinforcement aid you in your efforts to reach beyond your comfort zone?

3. How has praising others in the past encouraged them to be more cooperative?

4. According to the quote at the beginning of this essay, reinforcement is most effective when it is positive, immediate, and certain. How might this knowledge help you in your role as a leader or teacher?

CONCENTRATION
*Focusing Your Attention Will
Get You There*

WEBSTER'S NINTH NEW COLLEGIATE DICTIONARY DEFINES THE word *concentrate* as "to bring or direct toward a common center or objective; focus."

I once counseled a wonderful young female student who was attending Tennessee State University part-time. She studied part-time because her interests were so varied that she could not successfully carry a full academic load.

During our one-on-one session, her dissatisfaction with her present predicament surfaced. She finally admitted: "I want to graduate but my energies are so scattered. I am attending classes, working an evening job, and involved with a number of other projects simultaneously." After nine years at T.S.U., her frustration with the inability to complete the "college phase" of her life was beginning to take its toll.

> "The principles of war could, for brevity, be condensed into a single word— concentration."
>
> —Basil Liddell Hart

Our session proved beneficial. The outcome was cause for celebration. One Sunday, after church, my family and I were having brunch. To my surprise, this beaming young lady approached me at the salad bar: "Dr. Grant, please come over to meet my family. They have come all the way from California to attend my graduation," she urged me, hardly able to contain her excitement.

There, in the presence of her parents and a few other relatives, she gave me a wonderful gift. "Mama and daddy, this is Dr. Grant. A year ago, he wrote one word on a piece of paper that I kept on my desk. I read it every day. That one word motivated me to double my efforts to graduate. I just wanted you all to meet him."

The one word that helped the young lady to harness her energies was: FOCUS.

In their thought-provoking book, *Mission Possible,* coauthors Ken Blanchard and Terry Waghorn make the point of this essay crystal clear. Explaining the power of concentration or focus, they state:

> Human energy is like the energy of light. When it is dissipated, as in the average light bulb, it gets work done in an average way. But when that same energy is focused and concentrated in a single direction, as with a laser beam, it has the power to cut through any kind of obstacle.

Talk to the "geniuses" among us and you will discover that they have mastered the ability to focus their mental energies on a single goal.

Our lives are indescribably wonderful gifts from the Almighty. Each of us is endowed with the seeds of greatness that are our innate talents—even if we are mentally and physically operating within the realm of normalcy. The only way to cause a serious germination of these seeds is to decide consciously to *get focused.*

Napoleon Hill, an early human potential development expert, reminded us: "We become what we think about all day long." He was absolutely on point. We each get what we *focus* our mental energies on. The reason that concentration yields such bountiful results is found in one of the laws that governs the operation of the subconscious mind—the law of attraction. Our minds are mental magnets. They attract to us that which we *focus* our inner lenses on.

As the cocreators of our destinies, we operate in a field of pure potentiality. Our powers to create are activated by our persistent thoughts and strongly held beliefs. When we decide to block out the myriad distractions and channel our energies only in the direction of that which we wish to accomplish, seemingly miraculous things start to happen.

Many of us who are students of metaphysics believe that focused mental energy activates the powers of our superconscious minds, which many believe is a direct link to the Universal Mind of God. Why else were we told in Matthew 17:20 that "Nothing shall be impossible unto you"? What is faith if not our ability to hone in on some "substance not seen" but nonetheless "hoped for"?

Whatever you really want for your life is within your reach. Indeed, abundant life is your birthright. But you must *get focused* before you can go from "I wish I could" to "I'm glad I did."

Questions

1. Why do you suppose that "geniuses" appear to focus their attention effortlessly while perfecting their crafts?

2. In your dreamworld, what work would you do? Why do you suppose you would willingly give so much concentrated attention to the details of your life's work?

3. Think of the level of intensity you experience while playing a game that you find absolutely enthralling. How might you transfer some of that passion to other important areas of your life?

4. I often advise college students to choose careers that they enjoy rather than pursuing professions that promise big bucks after graduation. Is this sound advice? Why or why not?

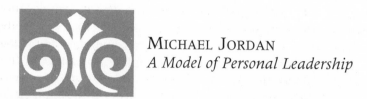

MICHAEL JORDAN
A Model of Personal Leadership

MICHAEL JORDAN IS A HIGH-PROFILE EXAMPLE OF WHAT IS possible when an individual decides to lead himself or herself.

The fact that he was able to muster Herculean effort during the 1998 NBA World Championship while besieged externally by the Utah Jazz (and their overzealous fans) and internally by a stomach virus, speaks powerfully about the degree of leadership that he routinely exercises. Moreover, he did so not only within the Chicago Bulls organization, but—infinitely more important—over himself.

Michael Jordan may appear to be a god to many of his worshipping fans and supporters, but he is as human as the rest of us (and arguably, more vulnerable than most).

What made Michael Jordan an enigma goes far beyond the fact that he was possibly the world's greatest basketball player. What makes him an incredible role model—not just for youth but for all of us—is that he has painstakingly developed the skills to lead himself.

It is now common knowledge that he was not good enough to make the team his sophomore year in high school. How he dealt with the disappointing fact of being cut from the team gives us a loose "rule book" on learning how to lead oneself:

Rule #1: When life knocks you down, get busy on a plan to get up. Getting up, however, is difficult if you do not give yourself a compelling reason to do it. That reason must come from your very core. Reasons to stand against overwhelming odds come from who we are deep inside. I am speaking about good character, the steel wall inside us that is formed by an endless array of personal choices that we make during the course of our lives.

Rule #2: To further develop leadership over yourself, it is imperative that you cease looking to others to do for you what you are capable of doing for yourself.

Rule #3: Insist on setting your personal standards higher—and higher. To paraphrase one great thinker, know that true success lies not merely in defeating the competition, but in outdoing one's former self. In order to set higher and higher goals and to surpass each preceding goal, one must exercise daily discipline over oneself. It has been written that none of us can afford to lose in this ongoing battle with the self.

Rule #4: The potential of your higher nature will be actualized in direct proportion to controlling the excesses of your pleasure-seeking, mindless, lower nature. To explain further, each of us has a higher nature and a lower nature. Like Michael Jordan, all the greats whom we admire had their daily struggles with the opposing drives of the lower self: succumbing to fear of failure, giving minimum effort, seeking the path of least resistance, and heeding a gravitational pull back to the comfort zone.

Rule #5: Stay focused on where you are headed. Leading a team that suffered injuries, suspensions, and a few embarrassing losses, Michael Jordan, entering the finals, led himself with the powerful affirmation: "We can win [another championship] with what we have."

The Chicago Bulls' splendid victory in Chicago on that Friday night was not merely about a team that had won more games than the Utah Jazz. What Michael Jordan taught us during the finals— and throughout the many years leading up to this point—was that *great leaders can inspire you. But no leader will develop your potential for you.* If you want to "be like Mike," you must become bullish about leading yourself!

Questions

1. In your opinion, what separates great leaders from the masses that they lead or team leaders from those who play on the same team?

2. Personal responsibility always demands that we look inward for all reasons for failure. How does accepting responsibility for our present lot increase the probability that we will improve what causes us dissatisfaction?

3. All successful leaders have a compelling vision that drives or pulls them to higher levels of achievement. What is your vision for your life?

4. *Passion, energy,* and *enthusiasm* are words we associate with great leaders. What can you become passionate about that will not only enrich your life but the lives of countless others as well?

THE SWEETEST "M&Ms"
Mind and Money

TO REITERATE A THEME THAT HAS THREADED MANY OF THE sections in this book, please allow me to revisit the concept of the subconscious mind. *The subconscious mind is believed by many metaphysicians to be the powerhouse that connects us to the Universal Mind of God.* We access the power of the subconscious mind by what we choose to believe strongly. Our deeply held beliefs are received as orders to our subconscious mind. It is a law—like the laws of thermodynamics or gravity—that what we believe at the deepest levels of our being will create real-life experiences.

What does all this have to do with becoming wealthy or acquiring more money? If an individual's finances are limited and his or her dilemma is perennial (the norm), the first thing that person has to do to change his or her financial status is to study carefully those orders (strong beliefs) sent to the infinitely resourceful subconscious mind.

Most of us say that we want more money when we want just as equally its opposite—to get rid of money (via shopping, gambling, perpetrating an image of success, or otherwise wasting it). *Bifurcated intentions will always yield fragmented results.* We either want to accumulate money or we want to enjoy what it can bring us now. So we must be honest with ourselves about what we want most— to have money or to spend it. If I want something and its opposite simultaneously, my confused orders to the subconscious mind can only reap confused outcomes.

So the first question is: how much money do you really want to have in your possession? How wealthy do you really want to be? I would maintain that regardless of how much cash you would like to have at your fingertips, you are already wealthy in those areas where you have focused most of your attention.

Here are a few examples: skid row bums have a wealth of "free time" on their hands; school teachers have a wealth of interaction with children; sports enthusiasts usually have a wealth of knowledge about the games and players that excite them; and individuals who love to gossip usually have a wealth of knowledge about other people's business. We are all wealthy in the ways that matter most to us. The same principle operates for accumulating more money.

When acquiring money becomes a serious priority, you'll notice that your subconscious mind will lead you to money-making ideas. Also, your subconscious mind will make you feel uncomfortable when you begin to spend frivolously.

So that you can begin to exercise more power of the purse, please allow me to ask you a few compelling questions:

1. Do thoughts of earning, saving, and investing money create pain or pleasure for you? Human beings usually work harder to avoid pain.

2. Do you have the "need vs. want" discussion inside your head before all expenditures?

3. How often do you purchase things to impress or to compete with others?

4. When are you going to purchase a home, start a business, or begin to invest a part of your earnings?

5. Do you focus most of your attention on spending money or gathering it; earning interest or paying it?

6. Normally, how much "free," nonproductive time do you have on your hands?

7. It has been said that we never allow ourselves to have more money than we feel we're worth. How much money do you feel you are worth?

8. What percentage of the people in this country became rich by luck or chance?

9. What limiting thoughts do you hold onto about accumulating wealth? For example, a very common one would be "money is the root of all evil." (Note: The Bible actually states that "The love of money is the root of all evil").

It is time for reorientation. You have been promised the abundant life. You *are* worthy of the best that you can honestly give yourself.

So go ahead, taste the sweet life that comes when you really understand the connection between your mind and your money, the sweetest M&M's of them all.

Questions

1. Why do you suppose most people spend more time complaining about their financial status than finding ways to improve it?

2. Do you believe that becoming wealthy will impair your relationship with the Almighty? How about family and friends?

3. Can you give yourself three good reasons why your net worth should more than double in three years?

4. Why do you suppose that spending money brings more fun than saving or investing does for many people?

5. In what ways are you already wealthy?

SLEEP
The Mysterious Reviver

LIKE SO MUCH OF THE WISDOM THAT PERMEATES THE writings of Shakespeare, his insights into the mysterious realm of sleep shed some light on a mystery that still confounds the minds of men and women today.

"Sleep the innocent sleep." Why does he characterize sleep as innocent? Possibly, because of its naturalness. Nature, governed by a higher law, induces sleep in its creatures, primarily to restore them.

The World Book Encyclopedia explains that sleep restores energy to the body, particularly to the brain and nervous system (perhaps this is why you are so irritable after a sleepless night). The encyclopedia also divides sleep into two categories, slow-wave and dreaming sleep: "Slow-wave sleep may help especially in building protein and restoring the control of the brain and nervous system over the muscles, glands, and other body systems"; while, "dreaming sleep may be especially important for maintaining such mental activities as learning, reasoning, and emotional adjustments."

Every essay in this book has concerned itself with the development of human potential through proper use and development of the human mind. There are virtually no limits to what our minds can conceive and achieve if—and only if—we pay close attention to the mind-body connection.

An old Roman maxim states: *Mens sana in corpore sano.* Translated, it means: "A sound mind in a sound body." Our minds depend on us to keep our bodies healthy and functioning at their optimal level. Our bodies need our minds to make the right choices.

> *"Sleep the innocent sleep. Sleep that knits up the raveled sleeve of care; the death of each day's life; sore laborers' bath; the balm of hurt minds; great nature's second course; chief nourisher in life's feast."*
>
> —WILLIAM SHAKESPEARE

Sleep is that blessed gift that illustrates how the mind and body are connected as one inextricably interwoven operation. So how is it possible to activate the potential energy stored in the human mind's power plant unless that mind has been rested through sufficient sleep (usually between six-and-a-half to eight hours per night for most adults)?

Americans are a restless bunch. We cavalierly burn the proverbial candle at both ends. We exhaust ourselves in a senseless search for excitement or, more tragically, to keep pace with God knows what.

All of the activity generated in the twenty-four-hour window of opportunity called a *day* oftentimes leaves us feeling uptight and weary. Our nervous system, trying to respond to every demand placed upon it, predictably becomes a little shaky. Just when we need sleep to save us from a multitude of injurious, energy-taxing choices, our nervous system also finds itself out of sync with nature's natural rhythms and refuses to deliver us from ourselves.

Many insomniacs admit that when calming thoughts and ancient beliefs replace a torrent of worries and groundless fears, sleep comes more easily. Further, it moves them effortlessly and naturally to that mysterious realm where they experience being washed in a "sore laborers' bath" and are soothed by "the balm of hurt minds."

Anyone serious about reaching his or her potential knows that a good night's rest is essential. None of our modern day escapist alternatives can replace "great nature's second course" and no amount of television, alcohol, drugs, gambling, or sex can substitute for the "chief nourisher in life's feast."

While you are awake, give all you've got to the challenges that await you. But as the day's productive activities wind down, so should you. Clear your mind of all troubling thoughts. Think of those things that make you happy. Forgive every slight. Count your blessings. Be grateful you got through the day. Consciously send thoughts of love to others. Then lie down to pleasant dreams.

Questions

1. Many of us, remembering that bedtime was usually forced upon us by our parents, subconsciously enjoy getting to stay up late at night. How might the "parent" inside of you take charge of the "child" inside of you so that adequate sleep can again become the norm?

2. How often do you use prayer, positive thinking, or cuddling to help you lie down to pleasant dreams?

3. Have you ever had a therapist to help you get better insights into your dreamworld?

4. Even with all the alarming messages from the mass media, what are some effective methods available for you to improve your chances for restful sleep?

5. Heavy consumption of alcohol or digesting certain foods (i.e., steak, ice cream, etc.) can undermine restorative sleep. Do you pay close attention to what you put in your stomach three to four hours before going to bed?

Conclusion
Staying Motivated for Life

AS I TRAVEL AROUND THE COUNTRY, I LOVE TO ASK AUDIENCES: "How many of you have had this thought enter your conscious mind at least once: 'there's got to be more to life than this' (i.e., what they are presently experiencing)?" Almost without exception, the vast majority signal that they have indeed wondered that there has to be more to life than what they are enduring.

I personally believe that the higher intelligence (consciousness) in each person leads him or her to the inescapable conclusion that life is a gigantic, enchanting, challenging, frightening, mystical, and downright fabulous drama in which each of us is a powerful and important actor or actress—even if we are not living life to its fullest.

The collective wisdom of some of the greatest minds throughout the sojourn of the human race seem to agree there is indeed a cosmic plan. They concur that some causal force is intelligently guiding the creating process and that human beings—wittingly or unwittingly—act as vessels and change agents through which much of the grand unfolding takes place. In a nutshell, man and woman partake in this cosmic play every moment. Our individual scripts define what we call destiny. Each of us acts out and codirects our own course as the plot unfolds.

Our destiny is the result of all our choices. If we allow ourselves to be guided by a higher consciousness, we get in touch with our cosmic purpose and the enormous power with which each of us is endowed. If we master the workings of our minds, there are no limits to what we can accomplish in this life.

It is to our distinct advantage to take control of the most powerful weapon that we have at our disposal in life's survival game.

> *"If I can conquer the demons from within, the demons outside can do me no harm."*
>
> —AFRICAN PROVERB

We now know how to take charge of our lives so that we are able to make optimal use of our time here, both for our personal fulfillment and to make maximum contributions to others.

We have discussed throughout this book how each of us has been programmed since childhood to think and to act in certain proscribed ways. We also sought to expand our awareness of how the human mind works, and how to use this new awareness to reprogram ourselves and rise above our usual thought and acting patterns.

Since this is a self-help, motivational book, the conclusion is designed to offer a few closing tips on how to stay motivated for life:

1.**Become aware that each of us has a self-concept. We cannot act contrary to our self-concepts**. In other words, we move unconsciously in ways that reflect what we genuinely think and feel about ourselves. For example, if an individual feels unworthy of wealth, a happy love life, the attainment of an advanced degree, etc., he or she will unconsciously sabotage efforts to achieve these goals.

2.**Notice that whenever you attempt to break with past conditioning (i.e., bad habits), uncomfortable feelings surface**. In his marvelous book, *Maximum Achievement*, Brian Tracy calls this human propensity to preserve the status quo "the homeostatic impulse," or the comfort zone.

When an individual decides to abandon smoking, to begin a physical exercise regimen, or to study with more dedication, he or she may feel a certain emotional discomfort or some degree of anxiety. Why is it important to know this? It's important because human beings are motivated every second to either approach pleasure or to avoid pain. But what is crucial is that we are *more* motivated to *avoid pain* than to approach pleasure.

Indeed, individuals with structural low self-esteem who are looking at life's possibilities tend to focus nearly all their attention on avoiding pain. Hence, a multitude of fears will surface when they meet with new challenges.

Achieving what we want in life is a simple matter of associating great pleasure with our desires and great pain with outcomes that are undesirable. If one wants to acquire wealth, familial bliss, or career success, the individual should focus on all the benefits and good feelings to be generated by accomplishing these goals. Anthony Robbins, a world-renowned motivational expert, calls this approach to behavior modification "neuroassociative conditioning."

3.**Always have a written plan with contingencies**. Know where you are going and how you plan to get there. Study options in advance. Prepare to be resilient. Once you begin to move in the direction of your desires, you will be met with resistance. Prepare psychologically and emotionally for obstacles. They are essentially illusory. They test your resolve and the level of your desire.

4.**Study your fears with dispassionate reasoning**. Someone once said: "Don't let your fears scare you." Fear, if properly understood and controlled, may well generate the energy needed to propel you forward. If fear is trying to trick you or sabotage your success, call it out and objectify it by writing it down and putting it in perspective. Motivational speaker Les Brown then advises: "Write down three reasons to get beyond the fear."

5.**Stop worshipping the god of other people's opinion.** Nobody knows what is good for you better than you do.

6.**Procrastination is either a signal that you do not know how to begin a task or that you are not sufficiently desirous of a positive outcome.** Analyze your reason for delay and get busy.

7.**Never forget that you are not a body with a spirit, you are a spirit with a body.** Your thoughts, feelings, and ultimately your actions reflect who you really believe you are and determine where you will ultimately go. Remember that spirits are invisible and uncontainable. Your mind, which connects you to the infinite intelligence of the universe, is obviously invisible but not so obviously without limits. So, decide today that you can live the life that you dream about and bring yourself to resolve:

"Nothing is too good to be true; nothing is too wonderful to happen; and nothing is too good to last."

—Anonymous

About the Author

It has been a real joy sharing these thoughts with you. My sincere prayer is that you will resolve now to do whatever is required of you to develop your God-given potential. I would be most grateful to hear how you are winning in the game of life.

Write to: Michael Grant
G&C Motivational Consultants
1026 1st Avenue North
Nashville, TN 37201
(615) 726–1934
gandccslt@aol.com
g-and-c-motivational.com